Field Tested

Recruiting, Managing, and
Retaining Veterans

Emily King

AMACOM

American Management Association
New York • Atlanta • Brussels • Chicago • Mexico City • San Francisco
Shanghai • Tokyo • Toronto • Washington, D.C.

Bulk discounts available. For details visit:
www.amacombooks.org/go/specialsales
Or contact special sales:
Phone: 800-250-5308
Email: specialsls@amanet.org
View all the AMACOM titles at: www.amacombooks.org

This publication is designed to provide accurate and authoritative
information in regard to the subject matter covered. It is sold with the
understanding that the publisher is not engaged in rendering legal,
accounting, or other professional service. If legal advice or other expert
assistance is required, the services of a competent professional person
should be sought.

Library of Congress Cataloging-in-Publication Data

King, Emily, 1965–
    Field tested : recruiting, managing, and retaining veterans / by Emily King.
      p.   cm.
    Includes bibliographical references and index.
    ISBN 978-0-8144-1779-9 (alk. paper)
    1. Veterans—Employment—United States.   2. Retired military personnel—Employment—
United States.   3. Personnel management—United States.   I. Title.
    UB357.K525   2011
    658.30086' 970973—dc23

                                                                              2011018173

About AMA

American Management Association (www.amanet.org) is a world leader in talent development,
advancing the skills of individuals to drive business success. Our mission is to support the goals of
individuals and organizations through a complete range of products and services, including
classroom and virtual seminars, webcasts, webinars, podcasts, conferences, corporate and
government solutions, business books, and research. AMA's approach to improving performance
combines experiential learning—learning through doing—with opportunities for ongoing
professional growth at every step of one's career journey.

Printing number

10   9   8   7   6   5   4   3   2   1

Dedicated to the men and women of
the United States Armed Forces
and the civilian organizations
that hire them.

Contents

List of Figures

Acknowledgments

THE CHALLENGE OF MILITARY TRANSITION and the importance of the topic to service members and to private sector organizations has been a professional focus since the late '90s, when I first began to explore it. Helping others to overcome the challenge and pay attention to the topic has become a mission that feels very personal. Several people have witnessed my journey over the years and supported me with enthusiasm, sure that a day would come when a larger audience would be just as aware of it and concerned with finding solutions. Chief among these supporters have always been my parents, Marty and Judy, who have always cheered me on in spite of roadblocks and frustrations. Similarly, my brothers Peter and David and sisters Mary and Philippa, along with their amazing children, have always been ready to listen, brainstorm, and troubleshoot. Donna, my cousin, best friend, co-writer of the audio course, and contributor to this book, played an integral role in the development of my thinking in recent years. I simply cannot imagine how this book could have been conceived or written without my incredible family, and "thank you" seems a woefully inadequate acknowledgment, but I'll say it anyway. Thank you.

Since the earliest days of my investigation, I have had the support of a few individuals who saw the potential and stuck with me through various versions of my vision for it: Matt Minahan, the professor and friend who oversaw my thesis on leadership styles of military versus business cultures; Sandy Mobley, friend, coach, and client who played a key role in my thesis and continued to cheer me on long afterwards; Rob Fleischman, my friend and business mentor, who maintained his faith in me and this work even when mine flagged; and Sherry DiStefano, the friend and colleague who helped me design the very first training program for transitioning veterans and who has helped to shape my thinking on the subject over the years; and Nancy Williams, who donated untold hours, ideas, and words of encouragement during the making of the audio course. Thank you.

My heartfelt thanks go to the many men and women who generously shared their firsthand experiences, giving me a window into the personal nature of military transition. Six individuals in particular have been with me since Day One of the audio program, allowing me to interview them and use their comments in various formats over the years, and who have been an informal group of advisors whose wisdom I have called upon for ongoing calibration of my ideas and understanding: Frank Ball, Jane Maliszewski, Bill Dean, Seb DeLiso, Derek Harris, and Karen Jeffries. Specific to this book, many former service members participated in interviews, surveys, and focus groups, fully throwing themselves into the effort to help their fellow service members going through the process of military transition: Donna Boltz, Matthew Donnelly, Randy Egolf, Luke Faber, Richard Goble, Richie Harris, Steve Harwig, Michael Hellyer, Kyle Johnson, Robin Johnson, Mike Lang, George LeFavor, Jeffrey Matthews, Robert George Mc-Cluskie, Michael McLaurin, Jimetris Parnell, John Pilat, Steve Raynes, Cindy Saladin-Muhammad, Art Schlussel, Frank Shawker, George Sneeringer, and Samuel Harold Stevenson. Many, many more have offered insight through the LinkedIn group Military Transition Interest Group, and I thank them as well.

Many civilian organizations supported this effort by making their employees available to provide insight, providing their perspective as employers, and otherwise helping me to do my work: Lynn Alba and Craig Henzel of Merck, Amy Mahoney and Claire Stock of L-3 STRATIS, Texanna Reeves and Betsy Silva of Sodexo, Amy Polefrone of HR Strategy Group, Eric Peterson of SHRM, Mike Elliott of Northrup

Grumman, Sean Collins of G.I. Jobs and Victory Media, Glen Williams of Walgreen Co., Christina Parisi and Andy Ambraziejus of AMACOM, and my neighborhood Starbucks where much of this book was written. Members of the media who covered my work include Karin Caifa of CNN, Morris Jones and Sara Kenigsberg of TBD.com, and Mark Stelzner of Inflexion Advisors and Job Angels. I'd like to thank a few other individuals as well: Les Garrison, Jan and Peter Bayer, Stuart Younkin, Chuck Anderson, Randy Epstein, Jacki Seley, Rand Gardner, Lauren and Scott Buttrick, and Colonel David Sutherland and Captain DJ Skelton for their insight into wounded warriors.

Finally, my heartfelt thanks to the many women and men who will go unnamed, whom I have had the privilege of coaching through their transition and who honored me with their stories, experiences, and struggles.

Foreword

EMILY KING IS A PIONEER in organizational development and a thought leader in "recruiting for retention," which means recruiting *lasting talent.* Her career spans over 15 years working on matters related to military transition, and she is highly sought after for good reason. Corporate hiring managers who desire to hire military veterans need real, practical insight on how to find, integrate, and retain this skilled labor force.

Employees with military experience are in great demand by the world's leading companies for their diverse training background and perspective, training that cannot be replicated in a corporate setting. This is where Emily's advice is especially powerful as she frames the role of hiring managers as *translators of culture.* She skillfully illustrates how best to increase an organization's capacity to on-board military talent, while accelerating and increasing retention of former-military employees in civilian/commercial environments.

Throughout her work Emily presents employee-survey data to support the notion that people *leave managers, not companies,* a key tenet that should serve as a wake-up call to all leaders in charge of diverse teams of people. Thus, retaining high-caliber employees is not isolated to the labor pool of military veterans, but is a challenge that spans every talent segment. Through an examination of best practices Emily shows managers how best to facilitate retention of talent within an organization with a keen focus on the cultural transition from military to civilian employment, key leadership differences between military and civilian organizations, and how to recalibrate the expectations of all concerned.

Our organization and Emily share many philosophies about human talent and the value of military experience. Her teachings and insights summarize more than a decade of lessons garnered from life in the HR trenches and are invaluable to all managers focused on bringing *lasting talent* to their organizations.

Sean Collins
Navy veteran and Senior Brand Manager, *G.I. Jobs* magazine
Publisher of the annual *Top 100 Military Friendly Employers*®
www.gijobs.com

Premise

PEOPLE OFTEN ASK HOW I CAME TO BE SO INTERESTED and involved in the subject of military transition, given that I myself have never served. In fact, I once had a senior military officer ask why he should take the time to meet with me, since I wasn't military and hadn't experienced the transition personally. My response to him was, "Sir, is there anything you need to know about the military that anyone could tell you at this point, given your seniority? On the other hand, are there perhaps a few things you'd like to know about the civilian workplace before your upcoming retirement?" I believe his response was along the lines of, "Fair enough, get on my calendar."

As for how I came to this field of study, it's kind of a funny story and generally a bit unexpected. I'll take a moment to share it with you. Many years ago, in my role as an organizational development consultant, I was asked by a large defense contracting firm to figure out why staff members were leaving one particular division in droves. It was around the time of the dot-com boom and techies everywhere were job hopping for all kinds of reasons like money and the promise of getting in on the ground floor with a start-up. Poaching was flagrant and it was not unusual for someone with technical expertise to receive astoundingly high salary offers and signing bonuses to jump to another company. Against this backdrop, the strong hypothesis was that the market climate accounted for the company's spike in attrition.

The first step was to prove or disprove that attrition in the division was higher than in other divisions and the company at large. A simple scan of the human resources information system (HRIS) showed attrition to be markedly higher in the division in question than in the rest of the organization. So far, I was neither surprised nor intrigued. However, I proceeded with demographic analysis of those employees who had recently left this group and, again not surprisingly, found that those who had chosen to leave were in their twenties and thirties with educational backgrounds focused on technology.

The next step in my organizational diagnostic was to gain insight into employees' reasons for leaving the company. Through employee focus groups and analysis of exit interview data I discovered something mildly interesting: staff members had not left this group to pursue brighter opportunities elsewhere (although they undoubtedly found them). They left because they didn't like their managers.

Today that's old news; studies have clearly shown that people leave managers, not companies. Managers come in all shapes and sizes, with varying degrees of experience and training. As a result, effectiveness among those in management levels tends to be uneven. My own studies over the years have shown manager effectiveness to be the number one lever for increasing staff satisfaction and retention, so its impact cannot be underestimated.

But let's get back to my attrition study. I asked myself, "What do the managers have in common that may be contributing to unusually high attrition?" The answer to this question was unexpected: In every case, the manager was a recently retired military officer. Now *that* was interesting!

The result of this study was a set of programs designed to smooth the cultural transition from military to civilian employment, to educate everyone as to the key leadership differences, and to recalibrate expectations of all concerned. Additionally, the programs aimed to accelerate the learning curve of former officers coming into the organization in management roles. Finally, one of the programs familiarized nonmilitary employees with various aspects of military culture and operations. So it was not just focused on "fixing" the managers but, more inclusively, on raising awareness at the organization level.

In recalling this project, I still to this day admire the company's curiosity and commitment to finding the root cause of its attrition. Acting on an apparent trend is common, but investing in an effort to truly understand it is not; it is, in my experience, most uncommon. The outcome provided measurable return on that investment by implementing solutions that resolved the core issue and improved the work lives of many.

And this is where my own curiosity was piqued. I went on to write my Organization Development master's thesis on the differences between military leadership and civilian leadership. This study compared findings from the previous one described above to the broader industry of defense consulting. I discovered the transition challenges and impacts to business were common to many companies, not unique to the first organization I studied. In many cases, the themes were strong enough to form the basis of predictions of future events.

I keep a live survey open online that continually updates data on the military transition experience, and I've noticed an interesting dynamic. There is a survey question that asks service members to rate their readiness for the business world along a number of dimensions, such as business acumen, sales and business development, cultural transition, etc. Respondents are sorted into two categories: general officers *preparing to leave military service* (Group A), and retired general officers who *have already made the transition to civilian employment* (Group B). Group A is asked to *anticipate* and Group B is asked to *recall* with the wisdom of hindsight as they answer their respective version of the question.

Interestingly, Group A—consisting of those anticipating the transition—has a higher level of confidence in its readiness than Group B—consisting of those asked to recall how ready they actually were upon leaving service. Among the group lacking civilian experience, no one reported having "no knowledge" (or, put another way, all reported some level of knowledge) of the areas queried. Further, several in this group assessed their knowledge at the "expert" level. In contrast, some in the group of *experienced civilians* reported leaving the military with no knowledge at all, and no one in this group said they came in as an expert.

My interpretation of these findings is that there exists a gap in perceived and actual readiness for the civilian business world. Practically speaking, this illustrates what so many veterans have told me: "I didn't know what I didn't know." Appreciating the significance of the military-to-civilian transition gives you an automatic edge over the many employers out there who don't take the time to consider it.

In contrast, the themes I've noticed among former enlisted personnel and those with shorter periods of service reflect a bit of under-confidence. For example, they may:

- Be unaware of what they bring to the table.
- Be unable to translate their military experience into terms meaningful to civilians.
- Have difficulty appreciating their own individual impact, since their military experience focused on the team as a unit.
- Have difficulty seeing the value and uniqueness of their experiences because, in the military, everyone around them had the same value and were not viewed in terms of uniqueness.
- Be less confident talking about themselves, less inclined to toot their own horns.

Fifteen years working on matters related to military transition have produced tremendous insight and a substantial database of success factors and derailers. In that time, I have had the privilege of working with many individuals and groups to overcome and head off challenges associated with the transition from military to civilian employment. While every situation has unique characteristics, the aim is always the same: to increase the organization's capacity to make veterans successful, while accelerating and increasing retention in civilian/commercial environments.

This has been a fascinating and fulfilling journey through uncharted territory, and I am grateful to the individuals and organizations that have given me a glimpse into their worlds. It takes humility, courage, and a commitment to excellence to invite an outsider like me to come in to look at what isn't working and change it. It has been exciting to see individuals who once struggled thrive and to see organizations that once had a revolving door of veterans become established in the military community as great places to work. Above all, I am grateful to those who serve or have served in the United States Armed Forces, and I remain committed to their success as civilians.

Introduction

THIS BOOK IS WRITTEN for organizational leaders, managers, and human resource professionals, all of whom play an essential role in an employee's decision to stay or to go. I want to distinguish the book from my audio course for veterans themselves, titled "Your Military Transition™," which speaks directly to the individual veteran about some of the same topics you'll read here. The audio course is intended as a self-paced learning tool for job seekers or new-hires transitioning from military service to civilian employment.

Throughout the book you'll hear me refer to "recruit for retention," which means recruiting for *lasting talent* versus recruiting for immediate relief followed by recruiting to replace those who were hired and quit. I use a variety of terms to refer to the veteran, such as "veteran," "service member," and "military new-hire." These are interchangeable. The reason for using multiple terms is that many civilians and veterans alike do not relate to the word "veteran." It seems to bring to mind World War II, Korea, and Vietnam, and isn't easily relatable to the gulf wars. Therefore, in an effort to be inclusive, I have provided alternative terms, and I hope it doesn't confuse readers.

Another term you'll see is "veteran-friendly." It refers to organizations that deliberately set out to attract and retain veterans. They invest, to varying degrees, in programs and marketing meant to brand them in the job market as welcoming to service members. Currently there are a relative handful of companies hitting it out of the park in this regard, but I hope and expect to see an increase with the availability of this book.

The book's primary objectives are to increase your organizational capacity by:

- Anticipating and heading off challenges related to the military-to-civilian transition
- Gaining maximum leverage from the strengths brought by military service members
- Positioning them for success in your organization.

These are three important drivers of satisfaction and retention among military hires, and they are your keys to success as a veteran-friendly employer of choice. Further, the book is aimed at increasing your own professional capacity as *a translator of culture and master of making the implicit explicit*. You will learn all about this concept as the book continues. Whether you are an organizational leader, line manager, or internal human resource professional, stepping up to the translator role will set you apart from your peers and directly impact the retention of your top talent. Many of the concepts and suggestions in the book apply to any and all new-hires and will strengthen your organization across the board. That said, my particular interest is in the success of veterans, so I'll leave it to you, the reader, to broaden the context to include other new-hires.

Throughout the book you will see quotes from former service members who share their personal experiences with the transition from military service to civilian employment. I personally interviewed and surveyed each of these individuals, who represent all branches of military service and both enlisted and officer ranks. All quotes are from former service members, no longer on full-time active duty.

Periodically, you will find what I call "Coaching Conversations," which attempt to bring real issues to life through dialogue while illustrating the value of using a coaching approach as an alternative to direct feedback. These are based on real situations, although names and identifying details have been changed to honor confidentiality with those who have generously offered to share their civilian challenges.

Part 1 of the book focuses on introducing you to general concepts related to military veterans entering the civilian workplace, to get you up to speed so you can move from understanding to action. Specifically, we'll talk about the unique strengths military service members bring to the civilian workplace. Then we'll delve into key cultural differences between military and civilian organizations. The natural thing to do after this is look at some of the common challenges veterans have making a smooth transition from one culture to the other. Finally, we'll look at what veterans need in order to have the same shot at success as other employees, which presents the notion that veterans entering the civilian workplace is, at heart, a matter of diversity and inclusion.

Part 2 builds on this foundational knowledge by introducing a model of military transition that can be used as a tool by hiring managers and HR professionals for understanding and anticipating needs, and by the service member to structure the transition experience and provide a sense of what's to come. I developed the model, called the Military Transition Framework™, after many years working with veterans and their civilian employers. The four chapters in this section focus on an overview of the model, each of its three stages, and a conclusion that ties it all together. Far from theoretical, the model is meant to be a practical tool, and this portion of the book is written to be put to work.

Part 3 introduces the Veteran Retention Lifecycle™ as an organizing structure. There are chapters on recruitment, on-boarding, performance management, and career development. You'll see that each stage of the lifecycle represents a dual picture: a potential point of failure and a potential point of re-engagement. Wherever your organization finds itself on the path toward hiring and retaining veterans, this part of the book provides you with ideas and tools for making a positive impact on people and retention.

The best way to read this book is with this question in mind: "What would a veteran need in order to succeed and stay in my organization?" In other words, compared to the more typical employee (nonmilitary) coming from another civilian work experience, what challenges and opportunities does your organization or the civilian environment at large present to a military new-hire? If you are yourself a veteran or have worked with veterans, bring the material to life by imagining how things would have been different if you'd had the information and insight way back when. How can it be helpful now? How can you help your organization become more veteran-friendly and help yourself become a great manager and leader of veterans?

Another tip for readers is to take advantage of the opportunities to apply what you're reading to your real-world environment by completing the activities in the book. Doing this will quickly move you from insight to action.

My career passion is helping veterans succeed as civilians while helping organizations succeed as employers of veterans. I thank you for your interest in hiring and retaining those who have done so much to serve our nation. Enjoy the book!

Part 1

Getting Up to Speed

CHAPTER 1

What You Get When You Hire a Vet

EVERY YEAR THOUSANDS OF U.S. MILITARY VETERANS enter the civilian job market. In fact, the Department of Veterans Affairs projects that more than one million service members will transition out of the military by 2014. As an undertapped source of talent, this segment of the workforce warrants a closer look.

As soldiers (Army term), sailors (Navy term), airmen (Air Force term), Marines, and Coast Guardsmen have been returning from combat, there is a lot in the news about their challenges related to finding civilian employment and to coming back with certain war-related disabilities, both physical and psychological. In parallel, we're hearing a lot about civilian employers demonstrating a spirit of patriotism by launching recruitment initiatives for veterans and disabled veterans.

Unique Strengths

Let's start with a very basic question: Why hire a veteran? Because it's good business. Set aside all of the other considerations like altruism and patriotism and look at what they bring in terms of competence and productivity. There are some key characteristics unique to veterans. Even a young person with only a few years of service will bring ingrained qualities and values. So while this person may not bring a lot of professional experience or marketable skills, he or she can easily learn new skills to do a job. Contrast this with a young person with neither the job skills nor the work ethic, and the distinction becomes clear in terms of adding immediate value to your organization. Research finds these to be the most notable military characteristics:

- Loyalty
- Values
- Discipline
- Ownership/Accountability
- Leadership
- Strategy
- Diverse experience
- Bringing order to chaos
- Important credentials

Some of these may look obvious, but keep reading and you just might be surprised at how they reveal themselves and positively impact a civilian work environment.

Loyalty

For those who may not be aware of this, joining the U.S. military requires each and every individual to swear an oath of loyalty. This oath is extremely serious. Having taken the oath, many veterans are accustomed to behaving and observing others behave loyally toward their employer. Loyalty is the expectation, *not* the exception.

Any civilian new-hire has the potential to be a lifelong employee if he or she has a reason to stay. Effective managers who are genuinely concerned for the welfare of their employees are highly correlated with retention. In the military, a high level of involvement is ingrained in the leadership philosophy. For example, in the military, your immediate superior knows you, probably knows your family, and is concerned with you as a member of the community on and off the job. It is that manager's job to "take care of" the team, which can mean being brought into team members' personal lives, celebrations, challenges of all types. The sense of community contributes to loyalty and may be instructive to civilian managers striving for loyal employees and high retention.

Values

The military, across the branches of service, has a very strong culture, as anybody who observes it from the outside can tell. The military has specific ways of doing things, procedure and protocol, which are necessary to serve the mission. Most civilian organizations don't ask employees to put their lives on the line every day (or any day), but the military does, so it requires structure and rigor in order to minimize risk. Values are not platitudes but are a cornerstone of that culture. These values are baked into the operating procedures and language and are inherent in each individual member, who then brings them to your civilian organization. This is a tremendous asset of the veteran job candidate because, as you know, with the average civilian job candidate, you only have their word for how they operate. Do they value integrity? Teamwork? Working under pressure? Everybody knows to say those phrases in an interview, but what does a civilian new hire *really* bring with him or her? With a military service member, you can pretty much count on seeing consistent evidence of the values listed above in addition to cooperation, personal responsibility, and a can-do spirit.

Discipline

This characteristic is often associated with the military, but what does it mean? Does it mean getting up at the crack of dawn, running five miles, and cleaning the house before leaving for work in the morning? In the military, discipline means doing things the right way even if the right way takes longer to accomplish; it means following protocol to the letter to ensure consistent results, rather than increasing risk by improvising. As a civilian outsider, we can easily observe that the military culture places great value on discipline, expects to see it, and rewards it. Discipline is viewed as an operating principle, a way of being, the "right" way to get things done. Discipline is a character strength in the military that in the civilian world translates to employees you can count on to see a task through to completion and to do so under extremely stressful conditions.

In the words of a former enlisted service member, "The military attitude is, 'adapt and overcome.' There's nothing we can't do—it might take longer, but we'll do it."[1]

Ownership/Accountability

In the military, you are issued the tools required to do your job. It is your responsibility to maintain and account for those tools, and frequent inventory inspections ensure that no one is caught without the tools he or she needs. If a junior enlisted service member loses his wrench and then has to report it lost as part of the inspection process, the cost of the wrench comes out of his paycheck, unless he can replace it himself before reporting it. In either case, he is paying to replace the lost government-issued wrench. That's all there is to it. By ensuring that the individual has a personal stake in the proper procedures and protection of assets, each individual quickly learns to take time and care to protect those assets. The individual who loses his wrench once will undoubtedly take full ownership of the replacement so as to protect the asset. Ownership and accountability are characteristic of the military way of operating, and service members bring this to the civilian workplace. Finger pointing and avoiding blame are a coward's way out, and the "right" manner of dealing with errors is to own up to them. Many times it is the veteran in an organizational team or division who sets the example for others to act with greater integrity as well.

Leadership

Any length of military service—even just one three-year tour of duty—will include training and experience in leadership. Leadership begins in boot camp and continues throughout the career of a service member. When you stop to think about it, the one thing that makes the military run effectively is a constant pipeline of leaders at every level (rank) in the hierarchy. Nobody invests in leadership training like the U.S. military.

One outcome of this leadership culture is a consistent point of view from veterans that you won't get from the average civilian, who likely brings a tapestry of leadership training and experience. In the civilian workplace, people can advance into management roles based on business results (e.g., sales figures) rather than on demonstrated leadership skills and ability. There can be a world of difference between words on a resume and real-time, on-the-ground effectiveness. On the other hand, when it comes to military service members, you can be sure that they do have some degree of administrative management ability if not higher-level leadership strength.

Strategy

The size of the military and the scope of its mission mean that personnel, especially those with responsibility for squads or units, are exposed to large-scale operations. *Everything* is a large-scale operation, when you think about it. For example, moving five hundred people across the globe by sea for an eighteen-month deployment is a complicated process to plan and execute, but not uncommon in the military. For this reason, veterans can often conceive of strategy and change at a larger scale than the average civilian who hasn't led a complex operation with lots of moving parts. This is not to say that everyone comes out of the service with strategy experience, but they *have* been part of a huge machine, a huge organization, and they have been part of making it work. *Things that may intimidate or baffle civilians in terms of how to get something done are often less overwhelming for a veteran.*

Diverse Experience

Military service members typically change jobs and/or locations every three years. You may hear this referred to as a change of duty station. Some describe the three-year tour this way: year one is learning the job and the boss, year two is mastering it, and year three is thinking about the next tour and training your replacement. In this regard, a military resume and skill set can look completely different from that of a civilian because it may reflect many unrelated roles that aren't connected on what looks like a coherent career path. For example, someone may have worked a personnel-related job for three years and then moved to a logistics role for the next three years, followed by three years of combat preparation and deployment. So when you're looking at new-hires and how they need to be on-boarded and what their world view is coming in, most will bring a variety of skills and experience that enhance their value to your organization, not to mention the flexibility to move and change roles as needed. We will talk more about this in Chapter 10 on recruitment.

In addition to diverse work experience, veterans are accustomed to working with a diversity of people. The U.S. military is demographically diverse, with representation from every ethnic and socioeconomic group and a strong track record of women and minorities in leadership. The military's life-and-death mission breaks down social barriers and creates camaraderie where you might not find it in the civilian workplace.

Bringing Order to Chaos

This is in some ways a summary of all previous strengths. Military service members often have experience working with lots of moving parts that need to be organized. This includes structuring processes and coordinating large groups of people. This allows them to envision order where someone else might be overwhelmed by all that has to be done. For example, consider a team that doesn't communicate or get along and that misses deadlines and has a reputation for being difficult to work with. To the average manager, this can look like one big nightmare to deal with. A veteran, on the other hand, might look at it and immediately see a path to order and getting things on track. A veteran may not know how to tactically accomplish it in a new organization, but he or she will likely be able to visualize an outcome based on the diversity of experiences that were part of military service.

Important Credentials

The military heavily invests time and money toward training service members. Consequently, many have received extensive (and expensive!) technical training and certifications. This represents a tremendous cost savings to civilian organizations that hire veterans. Likewise, many recent service members have pre-existing security clearances, which are of great value to government employers, defense agencies, and civilian organizations.

There are three benefits to understanding the unique strengths of veterans. The first is that you can leverage veterans as broadly as possible to serve your organization and to satisfy the veteran, who may not want to be limited to skills used in the most recent military job held. The second is that you can frame relevant interview questions, and the third is that you err on the side of making favorable assumptions about veterans rather than succumbing to unfavorable (and probably unintentional) assumptions based on stereotypes of the military (we'll explore this further in later chapters of the book).

The exercise on the following table is an important step toward identifying the gap between your organization's current culture and how it could be strengthened by hiring veterans. Consider taking a few moments to complete it and see what you discover!

Closing Thoughts

Our research has shown that former military service members bring great value to the civilian organizations that hire them, but that value is optimized when transition support is provided. Few organizations are currently providing such support. This is great news for you, the reader, because it means that you are ahead of the curve simply by reading this book. Implementing its ideas and best practices can truly differentiate your organization from others competing for military talent. It will mean a lot to job candidates that you and your organization care enough to learn about them as a community and have a strong desire to be an "employer of choice" for them.

The bottom line is that when you hire a veteran, you stand to bring somebody into your organization who (1) is accustomed to having to get things done, (2) is resourceful, doing it with little thought to their own self-interest, and (3) keeps the mission and the organization in mind. This is a strong place to start, regardless of the cultural learning curve that may follow. After all, think about all the resources of time and money organizations spend in an effort to instill those qualities in their employees. There are incentive programs, motivational giveaways and prizes, team-building events that attempt to engender a sense of commitment to the organization and to the work itself . . . all with various degrees of effectiveness. In contrast, the military cultivates an extraordinary degree of employee engagement without such extras, and the service members you hire bring that high level of engagement with them. Your challenge is to sustain engagement by having a veteran-friendly culture. This brings us to our next topic: cultural differences between military and civilian organizations and how to bridge the gap.

FIGURE 1.1

Putting It All Together

How Will Your Organization Take Advantage of the Innate Strengths of Military Personnel?

Strength	How Does This Quality Currently Exist in Your Organization?	How Can This Quality Strengthen Your Organization?
Loyalty		
Values		
Discipline		
Ownership/ Accountability		
Leadership		
Strategy		
Diverse Experience		
Bringing Order to Chaos		

CHAPTER 2

It's All About Culture

IT'S NO SURPRISE THAT MILITARY SERVICE MEMBERS come to the civilian workforce with a unique mindset. As a result, the transition from one organizational culture to the other is often fraught with missteps or, to put a positive spin on it, "on the job training." A manifestation of this transition challenge is that military service members may not ask for help or seek resources because they aren't aware of a need. Absent information or feedback to the contrary, they may see their methods as being effective when they are not. This creates an imperative for line managers and internal HR professionals to be prepared to provide proactive support. A smooth and successful transition contributes directly to success and retention, as evidenced by the most common reasons veterans give for leaving a civilian job: lack of fit and difficulty adapting to new ways of doing things.

The Challenge of Cultural Transition

Imagine leaving your retirement party after twenty years with a civilian company. You have a lot to show for those twenty years and a lot to be proud of. You also have another ten years to work if you so wish. You decide to join the military as a senior leader with deep functional expertise in the field of learning and development. You look forward to the challenge of implementing your proven best practices in a new organization. It is your first day. Your new boss greets you. Do you know what to call her? Jane? Mrs. Smith? Ma'am? With her is your new assistant. What do you call him? Private? Joe? Deputy? Kiddo, because he looks so young?

After a while, you are asked to prepare a simple memo regarding a routine training policy. Do you know how to write so people will understand it and take action? Do you use a casual, friendly tone? Collegial? Or formal . . . perhaps using a standard format of some kind?

As the lunch hour approaches, you are feeling good about the work you've accomplished on the policy memo and you are looking forward to sending it off to your boss. You attach it to an e-mail, which you close with "Best," and your name. Fortunately she knows you're on a learning curve, so she isn't too irritated when she comes into your office with a hard copy of the e-mail and the comment, "This is not appropriately written. You need to close with 'V/r,' meaning Very Respectfully, then your name. Oh, and if the person you're e-mailing is a peer, it is just 'r/.' And if you are e-mailing subordinates, drop the 'r/.'"

What a downer. You've gotten your first bit of corrective feedback before your policy memo even got reviewed. You have many very basic questions and it isn't even noon. This job change is going to be much harder and take far longer than you or anyone else had expected. Already you may have inadvertently demoted your boss and insulted your assistant just by the way you addressed them. Never mind the nuances of working in this particular division; it feels as though you have been dropped into another world entirely.

This scenario is unlikely to happen in real life. For one thing, the military does not generally hire professionals from industry in mid-career. Reverse the scenario, however, and you have a glimpse of the awkward transition from military service into civilian employment.[1]

Military Culture

Veterans are unique because of the military's specific culture. This should not in any way be viewed as a negative. Approximately two hundred thousand service members transition to veteran status each year, according to the Department of Veterans Affairs. Of the many who continue to work, they will likely start new careers in the civilian workforce, whether in the private sector or government. On-boarding and engaging these employees provide some unique challenges and opportunities for organizations.

Think about the concept of boot camp. Not only is it a familiar term among civilians, it is part of our lexicon that suggests intensive training and/or indoctrination. Every military service member—active or veteran—has gone through some form of rigorous training, most often boot camp.* Because the military's mission requires great personal sacrifice, the culture must be regimented and unambiguous. There are established ways of doing things and standard operating procedures and infrastructure to ensure they are consistently observed. There are absolute norms and expectations about worthiness, professionalism, and subordination, among other things. Lives are at stake and the risks are too high for anything less than full compliance. Boot camp integrates these absolutes into automatic responses, creating a sense of communal responsibility and an "all for one and one for all" attitude. This is very different from the civilian workplace, which to veterans can look like "*me* for me and *you* for me." In the words of one former Army officer: "In the military you expect to go to work and see your friends. You look to the left and look to the right and see family. In civilian organizations, you look left and right and they're thinking about working their 8-hour shift and going home. They don't care about you."

The manner in which work is accomplished is also strikingly different in civilian organizations compared to the military. For example, many veterans observe that *how* work is accomplished can be as impor-

---

*Boot camp is for enlisted personnel, while officers attend another program called officer candidate school (OCS).

tant to civilian employers as—maybe even more important than—*what* is being accomplished. This is counterintuitive to those coming from a mission-driven culture such as the military. Furthermore, many veterans find it distasteful. This can have impact on a veteran's level of engagement with his or her civilian employer because it tugs at personal values regarding good uses of time and activity.

> "The biggest lesson I've had to learn as a results-driven person is that, in the civilian world, *how* you accomplish something is just as important as the merit of the accomplishment itself. I went from being an infantry captain in the Marine Corps to being the only male in an all-female HR department at the hospital where I work. Needless to say, I was bound to make a few mistakes."
>
> —OFFICER, USMC[2]

Organizational Mission

The discussion of cultural differences between the military and civilian workplace must begin with a discussion of mission. Mission dictates military culture; after all, the military has the most compelling of missions: protecting the nation and its allies. The fact that each and every member knows and is committed to this mission drives everything about the organization's culture. The culture *has* to support the mission because of what is at stake.

> "In the military, mission always comes first. You definitely try to take care of your people, but it's always, "get the mission done regardless of the impact to the people." For some folks in the military, that actually means putting people's lives at risk that work for you. What I have found in this [civilian] world is, mission is important but it's not always number one. It's more important that you look at the long view, even at some points of not accomplishing your mission. It's kind of losing a battle but still winning the war. That's the biggest difference I saw and the biggest challenge."
>
> —OFFICER, USAF[3]

In the military, "mission" means something tangible and specific. For example, the mission of the U.S. Air Force is to fly, fight, and win in air, space, and cyberspace. These few words capture what the organization is there to do, how it will be accomplished, and where. All other tasks and activities are informed by this mission. It is a touchstone.

Military Mission Statements

U.S. Army

Identify high-potential leaders and provide them developmental opportunities to strengthen their executive competencies, equipping the Fellows to function as dynamic leaders who are experts in the business of running the Army.

U.S. Navy

The mission of the Navy is to maintain, train, and equip combat-ready naval forces capable of winning wars, deterring aggression, and maintaining freedom of the seas.

U.S. Air Force

The mission of the United States Air Force is to fly, fight and win . . . in air, space, and cyberspace.

U.S. Marines

Marines are trained and equipped for offensive amphibious employment and as a "force in readiness."

U.S. Coast Guard

We protect life and property at sea, enforce federal laws and treaties, preserve marine natural resources, and promote national security interests.

After reading the military mission statements, you may recognize some similarity to those of nonprofits, cause-related organizations, and some government entities. Here are a few examples of nonprofit mission statements:

> To enhance the quality of life in our City by working in partnership with the community and in accordance with constitutional rights to enforce the laws, preserve the peace, reduce fear, and provide for a safe environment.

> To improve the quality of life through a balance between technology and nature.

> To serve equally our members, our profession, and the public by defending liberty and delivering justice as the national representative of the legal profession.

For the most part, these mission statements clearly identify beneficiaries as populations in need of their services, not unlike the military. Something else they share with the military is a core value usually shared by everyone who works there. To be successful and effective, employees need to personally believe in the work that is being done. Otherwise, who would do it? These jobs are incredibly challenging for a variety of reasons, and it is often the deep connection to mission that motivates people to do them.

That said, a transition from the military to a non-profit is not without its challenges, as illustrated by this recently retired USMC officer:[4]

"Note the mission of my previous job: 'The mission of the rifle squad is to locate, close with, and destroy the enemy by fire and maneuver, or repel the enemy's assault by fire and close combat.' And now the mission of my current job in hospital administration, 'To improve the health of those we serve in a spirit of love and compassion.' The two missions are completely on opposite sides of the spectrum, but the dedication and values instilled in the armed forces are the same ones that mean so much to an organization, particularly one involved in healthcare."

In contrast, while many businesses pride themselves on their values and service orientation, the main objective is to make a profit so they can stay in business. As a result, business culture is different and its mission statements tend to be less concrete and more multipurposed. They might accurately reflect the employee and customer experience . . . and they might not. They might be familiar and useful to employees and customers . . . and they might not.

Business mission statements generally include a purpose and aim, a listing of primary stakeholders such as clients and shareholders, the organization's responsibilities toward these stakeholders, and something about the products and services offered. Some business mission statements are simple enough to be understood by all. Others are purposely abstract and open to multiple interpretations. At the end of the day, though, regardless of the words on a page, the mission of a business is to stay in business and this occurs through profit. This is the meta-mission that drives business culture whether or not it is specified in the official mission statement.

When you work for a for-profit organization, the profit part of the mission is assumed as a matter of course. Certainly it is the desire of most businesses to strive for loyalty and commitment among staff. But in the for-profit world it may be harder to engage employees with the mission, which can seem abstract and irrelevant. Company profit, even if linked to employee salary, is a vague concept that doesn't always produce passionate dedication from workers on the ground. As a result, personal commitment among employees is inconsistent in the business world. This often comes as a troubling surprise to service members who come from a world that values morale as a key component of success.

Of course, a CEO would want each and every employee to have a personal commitment to the company. In fact, large companies spend lots of money on programs, events, and "SWAG" (stuff we all get) to encourage loyalty and commitment among employees. Compared to the military, the corporate world relies much more on extrinsic rewards such as bonuses, perks, and merit raises. Senior executives often have the drive to accomplish financial goals, but for the average worker, profit alone is tough to get excited about. In contrast, the military has the intrinsic rewards of service, patriotism, and protecting the nation.

I developed a model to illustrate how an organization's mission shapes its culture, operations, and day-to-day behavior. Presented in two parts, the model looks first at the military mission and culture, then at the civilian organization's mission and culture. The term "Observable Characteristics" refers to easily observed aspects of an organization's true culture, what you and I could point to as typical of the organization based on what we observe about it. Let's begin with the military.

The upside-down triangle pointing down represents military culture. The wide flat plane at the top of the triangle represents the mission of the organization. Everything is driven by that mission, down to the level of individual behavior, language, interpretation of events, rewards, and demerits. The military's mission can be identified in all

FIGURE 2.1

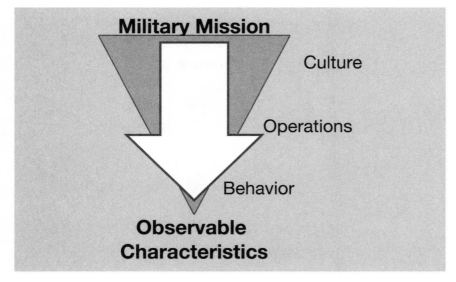

these aspects of the organization's culture, even down to the level of how every individual will respond in situations both mundane and extreme.

In the military, the mission is at the broadest part of the triangle. Mission sits on top of everything else, and everything falls out of an understanding and commitment to that mission. As the triangle narrows, the mission is concentrating through the organization and shaping behavior, events, practices, and processes to the point where almost anybody could rattle off a couple of stereotypical military characteristics like "hierarchical," or "formal," or "directive."

That's what the military mission—which is literally life and death—requires. In order for people to survive in that environment, everyone needs to be crystal clear about the mission, to the point that it is infused in every single thing they do. At the end of the day, service members swear an oath of loyalty to this mission, which may require them to put their life on the line. That's a pretty compelling mission.

Now let's look at the civilian organization.

FIGURE 2.2

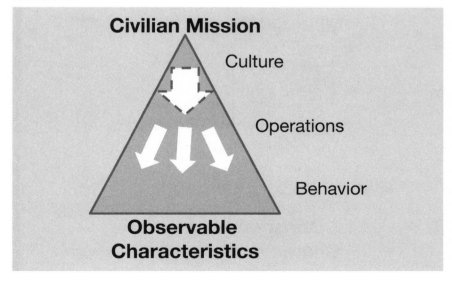

Looking now at the second triangle, we see the narrowest point at the top and the wide plane at its base. This represents civilian organizational culture where the mission still resides at the top but, unlike in the military culture, teeters on an unstable point. The base of the triangle represents observable cultural characteristics. Unlike the military's approach to mission, in a civilian organization a mission may be just words on a page. It may be the output of a leadership exercise intended to inspire and guide. It may be hung on walls around the office, embedded into policies and norms, or not.

As the triangle broadens toward the base, the mission can become diffuse. Fewer people may be able to recite the mission statement. Some might not even know what it is or that it exists. In fact, it is not unusual in the civilian workplace to find policies and practices in place that actually undermine the stated mission.

At the end of the day, behavior that an outside observer could see and name is highly individualized in most civilian organizations. The extent to which any employee embodies the mission of the organization will vary widely. Typically the more senior one's role in the organization, the closer one is to the mission in terms of understanding goals and how to drive desired outcomes. That perspective tends to diffuse as you move down through the organization. Here's how one former Army officer[5] described it:

> "On the operational side, you get a task. You finish it. You move onto the next task. You are in a comfort zone: 'I know the guy on the left and the guy on the right of me all had the same training. Our expectations are all pretty much the same in achieving a goal.' I get on the corporate side, I don't have that warm fuzzy of 'does the guy at the top to the guy at the bottom have the same goals for the company or the unit as a whole?' And are we going to get there in the same way? I don't know everybody's backgrounds and schooling, what they know, what they provide, and what value they bring."

FIGURE 2.3

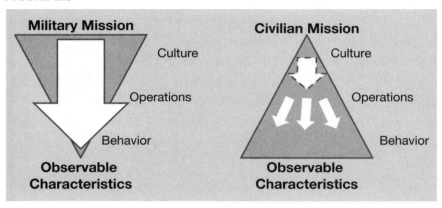

Remember the scenario earlier in the chapter in which you were dropped into a military job after a successful career as a civilian HR professional? You left an organization whose mission may or may not have played a role in day-to-day operations, as illustrated by the pointy tip of the civilian triangle above. You entered the military environment unaware of the wide flat plane of mission you now stood upon. Can you see how this basic lack of organizational context led to some of the missteps you made on your very first day? The military mission is served by the hierarchy of its rank structure and the expectations of deference and respect that go along with it. Things that may seem like trivial niceties in your civilian career—like how you sign an e-mail—can, in the military, actually be a barrier to accomplishing your assigned task because it disrupts the culture.

Military service members transitioning into civilian work environments experience a disorientation similar to what you would experience if you were dropped into the rigid structure of their environment. Here's how one former enlisted service member[6] described it:

"The chain of command is circumvented in civilian culture; elevating things above the boss, not respecting the boss. The impact is a breakdown in morale, in communication, and team unity."

Veterans come to the civilian workplace with an expectation that mission will be first, that they will stand upon a wide plane of mission-first culture. Sooner or later they come to the same realization you did in the earlier scenario: the basic assumption about what's important is inaccurate. Actions taken under this wrong assumption will, necessarily, rock the boat to some extent. Veterans can interpret this disconnection from mission as a lack of integrity on the part of the civilian organization.

As an officer in the U.S. Army[7] says, "Mission has to be broadcast all the way down to the janitor and, in the military, it is. On the other hand, I've had civilian managers say, 'Don't worry about all that. Just focus on what you're supposed to be doing right now.'"

Culture and Organizational Context

Compared to the military, many civilian organizations appear to have a loose structure that can look uncoordinated or even chaotic. Military service members are trained to bring order to chaos. How? By imposing command-and-control leadership. After all, in the military, "chaos" can look like people with guns shooting at each other, screaming, and running through the streets. Chaos in a corporate setting looks more like missed deadlines, unavailable clients, no time to prepare for a key meeting, staff away on leave, a messy desk, etc. Impose a command-and-control leadership style on this scenario and you may well see a spike in attrition!

The stakes are different. The competitive nature of the market requires agility in the form of changes to organization structure. You don't see that happening in the military. The military is what it is. It's got a structure that works for its mission and it stays true to that. So a common point of frustration about civilian organizations is, for many veterans, an apparent absence of leadership. For example, processes may not be consistently documented; people seem to be using any number of approaches to accomplish the same task, and with different quality standards. Some people don't even seem to know what the larger goal of the work that they're doing is. Corporate restructuring is common in civilian organizations, but can look ill-conceived and arbitrary to the veteran, as if nobody really knows what they're doing.

Without the benefit of a *cultural translator,* the service member may not understand in practical terms that civilian organizations need to be flexible, especially in a for-profit environment, and that learning occurs in real time, with real cost and risk associated with it. Certainly business strives to be proactive in anticipation of market shifts, but the reality is that business responds to market needs, and market needs are constantly changing. That's why organizations change their structures one, two, three times or more. They do whatever it takes to meet market demands.

Failing to comprehend the vastly different organizational context of a civilian organization sets a military new-hire up for disappointment right out of the gate. Time and again, I see this disappointment, even disillusionment, misattributed to the hiring organization when it should be attributed to the civilian workplace at large. The misattribution results in attrition and can be easily corrected by early education and expectation-setting on the part of the employer.

For example, a veteran leaves company A to go to company B, where the pastures are greener. Upon arrival he finds that some of the things he disliked about the first civilian employer are present in the second civilian organization, and maybe a third. It can take that third job change before the veteran sees himself as the common denominator in the equation. This can be an "aha" moment, or it can pass without notice. Regardless, it is at this point that the tacit learning accumulated from the previous organizations kicks in, along with a recalibration of expectations that is more realistic and accepting. For example, what looked before like a lack of values may now be understood as market agility. What looked like self-interest on the part of employees may now look like the challenge of balancing work with personal goals and priorities. What looked like a lack of leadership may now look like the complexity of managing in a changing environment.

A smart organization anticipates the risk of misattribution and sees the imperative to communicate organizational context early in the veteran's new hire experience. Any investment of time and resources will pay dividends in the form of accelerated performance and, one hopes, retention over time.

I recommend providing some level of transition support that doesn't have the company's footprint on it *before* sending the service member to standard new-hire orientation. For example, such support could include discussion of common success factors and pitfalls associated with moving from a military to civilian work environment, how to think about and prioritize around organizational mission, and basics of interpersonal norms in civilian culture. The timing matters because without some basics regarding the civilian workplace, organization-specific training is completely abstract and disconnected for the veteran. Return for a moment to the previous scenario in which you joined the military in late career. How helpful would an orientation to your new HR department have been without first being oriented to the Military?

> "The hardest part [of the transition] was deciding what to wear in the morning. After 20 years of knowing how to put on a uniform, dressing for the corporate world was a challenge!"
>
> —ENLISTED SERVICE MEMBER, USAF[8]

Lest you hear this statement in a negative context (e.g., downplaying the challenge of transition), see this comment from another former service member:

> "I would like to add one more piece of advice to the transitioning personnel. . . . Ensure that their wardrobe is updated and that they have at least two good suits. Otherwise, they will be scrambling to try and put together a wardrobe at the last minute and also probably have to pay out a lot of money."
>
> —ENLISTED SERVICE MEMBER, USMC.[9]

Clearly, this concern is very real!

Career civilians don't need this "basic training" because they've picked it up over the course of previous work experiences. Other things an organization can offer its employees who served in the military are awareness training for recruiters, line managers, and human resource professionals; individual and small-group mentoring; and self-study resources. This will be discussed further in Part 3 of the book.

The following worksheet is based on an exercise from my audio course entitled "Your Military Transition." To give insight to the military new-hire's experience, I've taken the liberty of consolidating a few responses for your review. Here's how they might respond to our questions:

FIGURE 2.4

Veteran's Worksheet

When I wore my uniform I felt *comfortable, part of a community, didn't have to always introduce myself because people could see by my uniform how to act and I knew how to act based on theirs.*

When I returned it at the end of my service, I felt *free at first, then a little lost. Felt like a loss of status.*

How do I communicate who I am now, without the uniform? *have to start over with every new person, takes longer, funny to see how people's tone changes when they finally figure out you outrank them!*

How do I identify who others are now, in a world without uniforms? *No clue! At first you try to figure it out by what they're wearing, but that is useless. Then you try to hear what people call them, but that doesn't work because, around here, everyone goes by their first name. Basically I just try not to make any assumptions and wait to be introduced. Hopefully that will tell me something about who the other person is in relation to me!*

What tips would you give newly separated service members? *Just hang in there, you'll figure it out eventually! Just try not to offend anyone in the meantime!*

There is humor and humility in the responses provided on the Veteran's Worksheet. This is a great posture to assume when making the military transition, as it makes learning easier than when we assume a resistant stance. We'll talk more about this in Part 2 of the book.

I use a metaphor based on sunglasses with my military clients preparing to transition into civilian employment, and it seems to help manage expectations. "Along with turning in your uniform, you also need to return the military-issued 'sunglasses.' You will be given a new pair by your civilian employer. Initially they may not work well because you're used to looking through the other pair of shades; things may look blurry, out of focus, you may even stumble around a bit. Expect that challenge and take it on with a spirit of curiosity." You may find this helpful with your own military new-hires, and I encourage you to use it or something similar to set them off on the right foot.

Key Management Skill: Translating Culture

One of the most powerful tools for helping service members accelerate their cultural learning curve is the ability to clearly translate your organization's culture into concrete meaning. For example, it might be self-evident that "teamwork" refers to working collaboratively, helping coworkers, and working together toward a shared goal. I'm sure it has greater nuance in your organization's unique culture. But in the military, "teamwork" can have additional connotations such as doing whatever it takes to get a task done, including working around the clock and expecting everyone else to do the same. In the civilian world of budget constraints, billability requirements, employment/work requirements, operational costs, and work-life balance, this may not be a realistic approach. (Recall the attrition study I mentioned in the Premise: it was just this type of misinterpretation of "teamwork" that led to so many staff departures.)What can you do about this disconnect? Keep reading.

Generally speaking, we aren't aware of all of the assumptions we make about what other people know or don't know . . . especially regarding things we consider to be obvious. As a result, key misunderstandings or misinterpretations only come to light after a mistake has been made. This can be a costly way of uncovering assumptions. To combat this, you as a leader in your organization need to perfect the skill of translating culture so it can be explained before mistakes are made. The good news is that I have developed a translator tool to help you make the implicit explicit by breaking down words, phrases, and concepts into behavioral terms. There are four steps to using the translator tool:

1. Select a *word or concept* used by your organization.
2. Interpret the word or concept according to its *practical meaning.*
3. Further break down the word or concept into *concrete behaviors* that exemplify it.
4. Articulate the organization's formal or stated expectations.

Figure 2.5 is an example, based on the concept of teamwork used earlier:

Now these are not textbook definitions and may bear little or no resemblance to how teamwork is thought of or measured by your organization. That is not important. What is important is to connect the dots between words a veteran is likely to hear, and expected behaviors. Your ability to connect these dots will have a very real impact on how long it takes new-hires to adapt and perform effectively in your organization's culture.

The exercises in Figure 2.6 at the end of the chapter on pages 36 and 37 leave room for you to insert words or terms commonly used in your organization.

Remember to use the translator tool to help articulate and support standards of leadership, and translate them for incoming military hires. Practice using it below:

1. Start with the word "leadership" as it is used in your organization.
2. Interpret "leadership" according to its *practical meaning.*

FIGURE 2.5

Translator Tool

Word/concept: **Teamwork**

Practical meaning: *work collaboratively with peers & colleagues*

Concrete behavior(s): *share information, be inclusive so that anyone & everyone who might be impacted by your work is in the communication loop, be willing to help others & to ask for help from others, avoid finger-pointing & blame when things go wrong.*

Formal expectation(s): *the organization measures employees on the following competencies related to teamwork: demonstration of helpfulness, ability to work cross-functionally, ability to work flexibly and adapt to changing work requirements.*

3. Further break down the word "leadership" into *concrete behaviors* that exemplify it.

4. Articulate the organization's formal or stated expectations for leadership.

Closing Thoughts

Consider this common scenario: A career service member—let's call him Steve—joins an organization and, among other things, observes an environment in which people watch the clock and leave at the end of their shift whether the work got done or not, or who have strict boundaries around hours they will and won't work or days of the week they will and won't work. These are all very new concepts to Steve, coming from an environment in which the norm is to do whatever is needed, whenever it is needed, to accomplish a task or mission. Steve looks upon this civilian environment and thinks, "Wow, what a bunch of slackers. I'm going to have to bring some order to this place." Here's how some of our real interview subjects responded:

> "I had let go of the expectation that I would be respected based on role/title. The employee attitude was, 'you can make me work but you can't make me work hard.'"
>
> —ENLISTED SERVICE MEMBER, US NAVY[10]

> "The biggest challenge was working with civilians who were more relaxed. A 40-hour week was half of my previous job in the military. There appeared to be no urgency to decision making. The mindset was an adjustment."
>
> —ENLISTED SERVICE MEMBER, US ARMY[11]

So begins the first culture clash, which is bound to aggravate all concerned. The clash is based on *a fundamental misunderstanding that civilian culture is similar to military culture.* The service member won't know a lot about this because he or she has not yet discovered it. Therefore, you must be the one to understand and anticipate the cultural differences so that you can effectively set and manage expectations from the earliest days of employment (in fact, before employment—during the recruitment process). This should be a two-way dialogue in which both parties voice their expectations and assumptions about what it means to do the job. It is only through such dialogue that core misunderstandings are revealed and, when it works, both parties learn from the exchange. The person quoted above is an Army sergeant. Interestingly, he demonstrated his own growing awareness with this advice to fellow transitioning service members:

"Remember that you are not in uniform anymore. You are not a platoon sergeant with 65 people looking at you, afraid to move until you say jump. If you don't remember this, you will not make it because you will be a Type A unpleasant personality that everyone wants to get rid of!"

Calibrating expectations is a necessary and ongoing activity, not only for new-hires who are former military officers, but especially for them.

FIGURE 2.6

Putting It All Together
Using the Translator Tool to Explain Culture

The first example uses the word Teamwork. The following exercises leave room for you to insert commonly used words or terms in your organization.

Word/concept: **Teamwork**

Practical Meaning: _____
_____
_____
_____

Concrete Behavior(s): _____
_____
_____
_____

Formal Expectation(s): _____
_____
_____
_____

★ ★ ★ ★ ★ ★

Word/concept: _____

Practical Meaning: _____
_____
_____
_____

Concrete Behavior(s): _____

_____

_____

_____

Formal Expectation(s): _____

_____

_____

_____

★   ★   ★   ★   ★   ★   ★

Word/concept: _____

Practical Meaning: _____

_____

_____

Concrete Behavior(s): _____

_____

_____

_____

Formal Expectation(s): _____

_____

_____

_____

CHAPTER 3

Common Challenges of Military-to-Civilian Transition

ALONG WITH THE UNIQUE STRENGTHS that veterans bring with them to the civilian workplace, there is a complementary set of challenges. Most of the challenges relate to the transition itself and can therefore be anticipated and addressed early on.

I have found the cultural learning curve to be the biggest challenge and the primary differentiator between those who successfully transition to civilian careers and those who struggle to find success. In fact, the cultural learning curve can take twice as long as it takes civilian new-hires to transition into a new civilian organization. Being on this learning curve doesn't mean the veteran isn't productive; to the contrary, quickly adding value is a strength common to veterans. What the learning curve means is that the nuances of civilian operations and interaction take longer to master. The key to accelerating the learning curve is a strong manager or mentor who, like you, takes time to understand and anticipate challenges veterans are likely to encounter.

An example of a cultural nuance that has tripped up more than a few veterans has to do with communicating about salary and earnings. The military pay structure is transparent and uniform (pun not really intended!), so talking and commiserating about pay is pretty common. There is nothing taboo about it in that culture. However, in the civilian workplace, it is often frowned upon and may even be a violation of policy to disclose salary information to colleagues and to get people stirred up about perceived inequities. The lack of transparency in the civilian workplace often comes as a strange surprise to veterans, and can be interpreted as a lack of basic fairness and integrity. This fundamental lack of understanding can create needless noise and unhappiness, yet is so simple to rectify by describing cultural norms early in the employment process.

Another good example of a cultural nuance is the notion of leadership. The military is known for developing leaders, and no one does it like the military. It provides opportunities and training for leadership that far exceed what many civilian managers and leaders receive. And, rightly, civilian organizations often seek out former service members for their leadership skills. *What most fail to consider is that these leadership skills were developed in the military context, which may not exactly fit their organization's culture.* Therefore, unless your organization's culture is characterized by a command-and-control style of leadership, the leadership experience of veterans will need some modification. For many, this is accomplished with time and feedback. For others, it takes longer to appreciate the validity of other approaches and to pick up on cultural nuances related to how leadership is expressed. In the words of one retired USAF officer:[1]

> "The military is very rank-structured. You are respected just out-right because you wear the rank. People don't know you from Adam, but they see the rank on your shoulders and you get respect automatically because of that. In the [civilian] world, that's not the case. Nobody knows your rank. You have to build that respect and trust."

I have identified five specific challenges that are common to former service members, based on my extensive work with them as they transition into civilian organizations. These challenges are organizational context, interpersonal style, management/leadership philosophy, tolerating ambiguity, and attrition.

Top Five Challenges for Veterans

1. *Organizational context.* Veterans have not worked in a context where their time and output had a dollar amount associated with it. For example, consider the former officer who is now a consultant whose time is billed at $500 per hour but who spends an hour trying to clear a printer jam because "someone's got to do it." The whatever-it-takes attitude is great, and all employees could take a lesson from his example, but it is also misapplied in this case because the value of the hour spent with the printer equates to $500 for the company. Perhaps the jam could have been taken care of by someone whose role had low or no cost impact. The point is that veterans come into the business world with a set of definitions around time and money that may not apply in a business context where profit and time are related.

Another and perhaps more radical change of context for the veteran is coming into a civilian world where employment is voluntary. They now work alongside people who can quit any time they want, or be asked to leave, and they're managing staff who can quit if they don't like the way they're being treated. Think back to the discussion of command-and-control leadership on the previous page. Not only does the approach keep things moving forward in the military, but it is also unquestioned because employment is contractual. Service members can't just walk off the job because they dislike their platoon sergeants. In the words of one enlisted member of the Navy:[2]

"I was surprised at the amount of personal freedom given to the employee on the civilian side. I had to adjust my working style and organizational skills to a world that required self-starters to be successful."

2. *Interpersonal style.* You've probably experienced firsthand the difference between *what* someone says and *how* they say it. It is easy to

misinterpret the content if it is delivered in a manner that is off-putting or raises defenses. In the civilian workplace, interpersonal style can be the difference between gaining the support of peers and alienating them, between motivating staff and intimidating them, between influencing senior executives and clamming up out of deference for authority. Interpersonal styles can be as diverse as the individuals in the organization.

The military, by contrast, ingrains an interpersonal style that supports its mission. The communication style is often described as terse, impersonal, and direct, because the mission of the military requires communication to be fast and clear. To acknowledge something someone has said, it is perfectly acceptable to say "check" or "noted." Those one-word acknowledgments are often perceived by civilians as dismissive. Feeling dismissed can quickly lead to a misinterpretation of meaning and intention, which in turn can damage relationships. Funnily enough, the attempt to be clear and direct actually creates a lack of clarity regarding intent. "I just walked up to the new guy's office door and informed him of a meeting this afternoon. He said, 'check.' What is that? Are we computers now?"

If your organization wants to integrate veterans into its culture, the solution is twofold: first, describe the organization's style of interacting and communicating during the on-boarding process and, second, raise awareness among all employees of the military context. Smart organizations are beginning to do this under the auspices of diversity and inclusion training. Viewing it as a diversity issue encourages everyone to be more effective, not just in the way they say things but in the meaning they choose to attach to what others say to them. Simple awareness training can head off a host of day-to-day misunderstandings.

3. *Management and leadership philosophy.* In the military, the leadership philosophy and approach evolves from the mission itself. What is your organization's leadership philosophy? Is it mission first? People first? Profit first? In the military, it is easy to understand why things

are done the way they are once you understand the mission. In civilian organizations, it may be harder to clarify the mission itself, let alone the leadership philosophy. This is another opportunity for strategic human resources and line managers to contribute by playing the role of cultural translator. How does your organization think about leadership? To what extent are these beliefs an abstract philosophy and to what extent are they baked into actual practice? What are some examples? If you were to ask yourself why managers and leaders do what they do, would you say it was to serve the organization's mission? To avoid repercussions? To keep the boss happy? To keep staff happy? To take the path of least resistance?

You may not have considered these questions because they seem irrelevant. After all, at the end of the day we just need to know how our organizations want us to operate so we can execute. But taking a moment to think about your organization's leadership philosophy (whether it is formally articulated or not) will help you explain context to your military hires. They will come in expecting leadership to be focused on mission, and they may disengage if they sense that leadership is focused on politics, self-interest, or other goals not directly related to mission. Explaining this context will help to set realistic expectations among new-hires.

During all the years I've worked in organizations and with former military service members, I've found that when they can get over this learning curve of how to apply their management and leadership skills in a civilian setting, they're outstanding leaders who are respected, enjoyed, and even beloved. That said, it's something for which they may need coaching, either through the on-boarding process or in leadership training.

4. *Tolerating ambiguity.* Certainly the military has its share of ambiguity, as any organization its size does. But the ambiguity veterans find in civilian settings looks to them like a lack of leadership. The ambiguity they are accustomed to tolerating in the military is what I would call *controlled ambiguity* because, yes, there may be ambiguity, but it

exists in the context of this super-structured organization and culture in which there are ways of doing things that are documented and followed. In the military, the point is to limit the degree of ambiguity associated with change by executing change in a stable and prescribed manner.

In contrast, ambiguity in the civilian workplace can be anywhere at any time in any form, manifested by anyone, and is often experienced by a veteran as chaos. "Why isn't anybody in charge around here?" and "How does this place stay in business, running like this?" are common questions asked by military new-hires. And they may be fair questions. But they do not provide insight or openings for discovery; they simply accuse. Asking (or even just thinking) questions in an accusatory manner is not conducive to success for most new-hires, military or not.

This again is an issue of expectation-setting, which should begin during recruitment and continue through on-boarding. It is setting clear expectations that are accurate, that don't make assumptions about what the veteran knows, and that paint a clear picture of what the veteran is going to be walking into and how daily life might be a little (or a lot) different than it was in the military.

5. *Attrition.* My studies of transitioning service members and civilian HR professionals suggest that many veterans leave their first civilian job within thirty-six months. It may take more than two job changes before he or she finds an organization that feels like a fit. Depending on the position, this pace of attrition can be costly to an organization in terms of return on hiring investment. For example, if you employ recruiters, place job ads or attend career fairs, conduct a few rounds of interviews with several candidates, make the hire and train the new employee, you are accruing costs. Even if you are not engaged in these particular activities, there are costs associated with turnover and discontinuity of service to clients while replacement staff come up to speed.

In other words, you are making an investment. The longer the individual remains with the organization, the more likely you are to recoup the hiring investment. This is a typical business model and applies to all new-hires, not just veterans. Data suggest, however, that attrition is higher among recent service members than among the larger employee base.

As stated earlier, surveys of former military and internal HR professionals identify "lack of cultural fit" as the leading cause of voluntary attrition. One reason for so many poor fits is that many service members don't or can't explore nonmilitary interests, passions, avocations, or career goals before accepting a civilian job. There are several reasons for this. Traditionally, service members:

- Work their jobs right up until the last day of service.
- Attend a brief transition training program, offered by the military, that focuses on resume preparation, job sourcing, and interview skills.
- Are encouraged to extend their contracts or, in common parlance, to "re-up" rather than separate from the military.
- Have been occupied with the twenty-four/seven military lifestyle, rather than exploring interests far and wide.

Many veterans have families and households to support, creating a real sense of urgency to maintain a steady paycheck by finding civilian employment right away, further hindering the discovery process. In a rush to secure civilian employment, they may accept an initial job offer rather than explore options. As a result, discovery occurs on the job through a process of elimination. While it is not your job to play life coach to the veteran, you want to be aware of this tendency so you can convey—early and often—the job and career options available within your organization. Wouldn't you rather have a valuable employee transfer internally than quit and join a competitor? Assuming that new-hires will know they can move around internally is a good example of an assumption civilian leaders are likely to make. Remember: in the military, career moves are structured and one can't skip levels or necessarily pursue professional interests. Often, service members continue along the path set for them by the military, based on personnel needs rather than personal interests. Consider the following coaching conversation between Liz and her manager.

Coaching Conversation: Cultural Challenge

In this scenario, Liz is seeking advice from her manager about staff management.

Liz: Thanks for your time today. I could really use your advice on a staff management issue I'm struggling with.

Manager: Sure thing, Liz, what's going on? [How would you describe your current performance challenge?]

Liz: I just can't seem to get used to how staff interact with managers in this environment. They have no problem coming right into my office with complaints or suggestions.

Manager: What have you tried so far to address the challenge?

Liz: Well, it didn't take long to see that reprimanding them for insubordination did not work. After that mistake, which I won't make again, I haven't really known what to do except listen and promise to take their issue under advisement.

Manager: How effective was that approach?

Liz: One person just kept bugging me about it until I lost my patience and barked at her. I just can't seem to get used to the lack of respect shown to superiors.

Manager: How is it similar to situations you faced in the military?

Liz: It isn't. It would never happen in the military. You could go to the brig for talking back to a superior.

Manager: How is it different here compared to the military?

Liz: Well, here, people have free will to quit if they want to. So if they are valuable employees, they kind of have you over a barrel. You, as manager, have no choice but to keep them happy, even if it means the job doesn't get done.

Manager: What have you observed others doing in response to similar challenges in this environment?
[pause]

Liz: I watch my peers, who seem to do a lot of compromising and accommodating of staff.

Manager: How effective is that approach?

Liz: It definitely defuses the situation if the employee is emotional. It also makes more work for the manager, though.

Manager: What could you do to more effectively address the challenge?

Liz: I would like to find a way to deal with it that doesn't necessarily add to my workload, but that encourages the employee to be part of the solution rather than just handing it off.

Manager: How would you see that playing out?

Liz: Good question! I think that after listening to the employee describe the issue and confirming that I understand it correctly, I could start by asking him or her for suggestions as to how they could address it. Or, like you just asked me, I could ask what they've already done to address it. That would train them to try to resolve it before coming to me in the future. And I could wrap up by asking what, if anything, they want to request of me in terms of assistance. How does that approach sound to you?

Manager: I think it sounds great. I try to use a similar approach with my direct reports so they try to resolve their own issues before elevating them to me, while knowing they'll have my support if they need it. So, what's the next step?

Liz: One of the analysts is on my calendar this afternoon to discuss an issue. I want to jot down some notes beforehand to remind myself of what to say, then I'm going to put it to work and see how it goes. Thanks!

Manager: My pleasure, Liz, let me know if you'd like to follow up on this conversation later.

Closing Thoughts

You are arming yourself with knowledge to prevent premature attrition and to increase organizational return on investment (ROI). Simply building awareness of what veterans bring to and find challenging in civilian organizations is a powerful first step. When we've asked internal HR professionals why they see attrition among veterans, they essentially say the same thing as the veterans themselves: inability to let go of the military way of doing things. You as line manager or HR professional have the opportunity to affect this trend by translating the culture and calibrating the expectations of all concerned.

CHAPTER 4

Military Transition as a Matter of Diversity and Inclusion

TWO YEARS AGO I SUBMITTED A CONFERENCE PROPOSAL suggesting that veterans in the civilian workforce be considered by diversity and inclusion professionals. To my surprise and delight, the proposal was accepted and I gave the presentation to a small but interested group. It was the first of many such presentations I would give at industry conferences, all gratifying developments.

Based on several factors, I see military-to-civilian transition as a diversity matter. At the simplest level—demographically—veterans are a diverse group. The most recent data available from the Defense Manpower Data Center is from 2008.[1] It shows that 14.6 percent of the active military population is made up of women, 17.7 percent is African American, and 7.6 percent identify as "other" than white or African American.

A deeper look reveals even more compelling evidence of veterans as a diverse group. Specifically, I have identified four criteria included in this sentence: veterans are *a defined group* (i.e., it is possible to say whether one was or was not in the U.S. military) that comes to the civilian workforce from a *strong culture*, with a *shared set of challenges* that *can positively or negatively impact their success* as civilian employees.

Self-Perception

A while back I posted an article on my blog on the subject of why the military transition is easier for some veterans than for others. I referenced two examples, loosely based on clients I've worked with over the years. In the first case, the retired officer recognized he was leaving one world behind—the military—and entering a new world—the civilian world. He acknowledged knowing very little about how to succeed or thrive in the new work environment. So he came in humble, expecting to feel like a beginner for a while. With defenses down, he was receptive to learning.

The second example offered a useful contrast. Also a retired officer who had achieved a certain level of officer status and left service at the peak of his career, he too had a number of offers to consider from civilian organizations. In fact, he really felt like he was the "It" guy in the market. He proceeded with an attitude of "I'm at the top of my game and you're lucky to have me." He was not open to learning, he was defensive about feedback, and he had a rigid way of doing things that allowed for no alternative approach. The stressful situation of being a senior leader in a completely new work environment seemed to amplify the worst side of some characteristically military operating styles. The more resistance he got from his civilian staff (which would be insubordination in the military and not permitted), the more dug-in this gentleman became. Things spiraled down to the point where he had alienated himself from his peers. Staff didn't like him and were beginning to demonstrate attrition. His seniors began to see him as a risk, unsure of his ability to make a successful transition into the civilian organization.

Meanwhile, the gentleman in the first example was developing a fan base. He experimented with being himself in an organization that didn't require regimented behavior. He had fun and so did his colleagues and staff. He was, by choice, on a learning path in which he made mistakes and at times even had to laugh at himself. Ultimately, this individual was promoted into an even higher level of executive

leadership while the fellow in the second example was given proba-
tional status and an aggressive "get-well" plan. In the end, not surprisingly, the man in the second example chose to leave the organization.

How could someone in your position have assisted the second
man? What would have resulted in a better outcome? We can certainly
make generalizations from these two examples, but what we want to
take away from them is that success is the responsibility of the individual new-hire and of the organization. An organization that understands the military context that a new-hire is coming from and has
resources, programs, or tools to assist him or her in the transition to
civilian employment will be more likely to retain military talent.

The tremendous difference in culture alone, between the military
and any civilian organization, can make it hard for a career service
member to succeed where another person would thrive. In the words
of one enlisted member of the USAF, "I knew I could do a lot more
than I was doing, but didn't know how to plug in to contribute more.
I got lumped in with other military folks, but we are all individuals."[2]

In many cases, the person or team within an organization whose
role it is to shepherd the success of diverse populations is referred to
as Diversity and Inclusion. Veterans are a group that can be measured
in terms of retention and positively impacted by initiatives geared to
their success.

Managing Assumptions

Individuals (former military or not) who have had at least one civilian
job accumulate a great deal of tacit knowledge regarding business operations ("tacit" meaning they gain the knowledge in real time as they
operate in the organization). For example, an hourly worker might
know to clock time at the end of the day and might simply need to
know the physical location of the time clock in a new job. If asked
how they knew to do this, they may very well shrug and say something
like, "Everyone knows you have to clock your time before you leave a
job site." "Everyone," in this case, would include those who had

worked in this type of setting before, and it would exclude all of those who had not.

Or how about choosing a benefits plan? Anyone who has ever worked as a civilian has picked up some do's and don'ts about this over the course of his or her career. But a veteran has never had to do this and may not have the first clue as to what it all means. Therefore, as an HR or line manager, you can make a real difference by spending time on this topic during or after new-hire orientation training. An easy fix is to simply expand benefits discussions with military hires.

I can easily imagine an exchange between a career service member and a civilian coworker. Let's say they are both new employees sitting side by side in orientation training. The veteran remarks, "I keep hearing about sign-up for benefits programs. What's that all about?" The civilian responds, "Oh, you need to get it done before the end of this week." After a pause, the vet asks, "Get what done?" The colleague looks at her with amusement and says, "What do you mean 'get what done'? Get your selections turned in!" Another pause. The vet: "My selections? Isn't that already done for us, or is nobody in charge around here?" Both walk away from the exchange perplexed, and none the wiser for having met.

Benefits are but one example. Veterans of almost any length of service have never had to negotiate for a salary increase, submit relocation expenses, build business, or contribute in any way to profitability. They have never had to place a dollar value on their time and manage it accordingly, let alone document it on a daily or hourly basis.

I am reminded of myself as a new college graduate from a tiny liberal arts college. Everything I had to learn about being a professional was learned the hard way—through the public embarrassment of trial and error. I remember some of the earliest feedback I received about appropriate skirt length and other such matters that are now common sense to me. Of course, I had an advantage when it came to things like selecting benefits and moving up the career ladder: my youth and lack of professional experience were apparent for all to see! The point is that as an obvious new professional, things were explained and taught to me that one might not think to explain to a veteran with a long military career. Please do not assume your military hire knows what to do or how to do it in your environment.

As a civilian line manager or HR professional, assumptions present risks. Things you might take for granted can result in performance breakdowns, communication gaps, poor working relationships, costs (both actual and opportunity), and high turnover, to name a few. Assumptions, too, can be considered a blind spot, like the veterans' blind spots described earlier. Everyone has a learning curve and just recognizing it is a tremendous first step.

Personal Bias

Talk of assumptions is a natural bridge to talking about bias in general. While a former service member may look just like you or me on the outside, he may represent very different things based on the values and beliefs we were each raised with or learned throughout our lives. The conscious or unconscious judgments we make of others shape how we engage with them, and although we might think we present a neutral expression, our true feelings are usually evident to others.

A quick scenario: Chris is a recently retired Navy captain who has decided to accept your firm's offer of a senior management slot. He comes in expecting the immediate respect and deference commensurate with his senior military rank. Does this expectation align with what Chris is likely to encounter as a new manager in your company? To the contrary, he may encounter people who don't care that he was a senior officer or who in fact resent him for it based on political beliefs. Some may simply disregard it as irrelevant. It would probably be a good idea for all concerned to have a degree of self-awareness about their respective attitudes.

I often remind transitioning veterans that the way civilians view them may be shaped by political views, news coverage, or movies like *Full Metal Jacket, Black Hawk Down,* or *Apocalypse Now.* The media doesn't do much to bolster an actualized professional image of the military service member, and a variety of unfortunate stereotypes result.

Most of us have some biases. What ideas and attitudes do you have about the military and its members? Put aside concerns of political correctness. We each have our impressions for a reason; they came to us through our life experience. Often we aren't even aware of our own biases until confronted by them, at which point we have an opportunity to look at them honestly in terms of their impact on ourselves and others and work toward being more open, as well as to support our staff and colleagues in doing the same, whether or not they are veterans. Consider the example in Figure 4.1 on page 54.

Diversity, Veterans, and Disability

A natural dovetail exists between a discussion of veterans as a culturally diverse segment of the traditional civilian workforce and a discussion of another diverse segment: employees with disabilities. As service men and women return from combat, we hear more and more about the physical and emotional challenges they sustain and what that means for them in the civilian workplace. The term "wounded warrior" has emerged in the public domain as a way of referencing this group, used by the Pentagon and industry alike. Hiring wounded warriors offers organizations the opportunity to leverage institutional knowledge and best practices related to disabilities with veterans in the workplace.

Headlines may focus on war injuries, but many who return from combat will not have visible injuries. For example, the "signature injuries" of recent and current wars are post-traumatic stress disorder (PTSD) and traumatic brain injury (TBI), which are invisible to observers (in some cases, TBIs may show visible signs). In an effort to clarify, inform, and dispel misperceptions, we have included below a few terms that can create barriers to civilian employers who might hire veterans. Potential employers of veterans, National Guard members or reservists returning with injuries are encouraged to recognize that they want to

text continues on page 56

FIGURE 4.1

Assumption Check-In

Bias/Assumption/Stereotype: *military veterans are rigid and inflexible.*

When/where did I learn this to be true? *Growing up, I had an uncle who made us do things a certain way and it had to be just –so, like if we borrowed his tools we had to put them back in the exact same place we took them from and he would get really mad if we misplaced or left them out.*

Looking at it now, what evidence tells me it is, in fact, true? *I have met lots of military service members over the years who were like my uncle in this way.*

What evidence tells me that it may not be true? *I have met several veterans over the years who were easy going and didn't care how something got done as long as it got done right.*

How can I check this out or learn more about it? *Notice the qualities of being rigid and inflexible wherever they may be, and pay attention to my tendency to assume veterans will operate this way. Ask if the person is open to other approaches and to negotiating.*

My updated view could be restated this way: *Being rigid and inflexible is not unique to military veterans. It is a work style I see in all kinds of people, and that I find personally challenging to deal with.*

My growth opportunity: *I can work on not being shut down by people who seem rigid and inflexible.*

FIGURE 4.2

Assumption Check-In: In Your Own Words

Bias/Assumption/Stereotype: _____

_____

_____

When/where did I learn this to be true? _____

_____

_____

Looking at it now, what evidence tells me it is, in fact, true?

_____

_____

What evidence tells me that it may not be true? _____

_____

_____

How can I check this out or learn more about it?

_____

_____

My updated view could be restated this way: _____

_____

_____

My growth opportunity: _____

_____

_____

work, assume their competence and ability, and assume the same hiring standards for all employees, including those with disabilities.

Post-Traumatic Stress Disorder (PTSD)

PTSD is an anxiety disorder that can affect people from all walks of life and that has been dubbed one of the "signature" injuries of the global war on terror. PTSD is a psychological health injury that can develop in response to exposure to an extremely traumatic event, such as military combat. It is characterized by vivid re-experiencing of the ordeal in the form of flashbacks, intrusive memories, and nightmares. Men and women with PTSD are often hyper-vigilant and may have difficulty focusing. While these issues do not necessarily affect work, they are important to be cognizant of as an employer. This does not preclude individuals experiencing PTSD from being valuable contributors to civilian organizations, and the opportunity to contribute is a powerful factor in their recovery. (See Appendix on Resources for additional employer resources.) Employers should consider reasonable accommodation for counseling appointments, considering these as necessary as any other doctor's visit. Again, PTSD should not be considered a barrier to employment, but more a condition that employers want to be sensitive to and support their employees' efforts in the recovery process.

Traumatic Brain Injury (TBI)

Traumatic brain injury is the other "signature injury" of the current wars. It is an umbrella term that spans a wide continuum of symptoms and severity, most of which will decrease over time. Symptoms of TBI can look similar to those of PTSD, but TBI is a physical injury caused by a blow or jolt to the head or a penetrating head injury that affects the brain. Many people with TBI (or PTSD, for that matter) won't face workplace problems at all and in fact benefit tremendously from the opportunity to work and contribute. Among those who do encounter challenges, however, symptoms may include headaches, vertigo, anxiety, short-term memory deficits, and limited concentration. (See chapter 10 for employer resources.)

Other Physical Injuries

PTSD and TBI have been dubbed invisible injuries because they are not visible or obvious. But now, because of the sophisticated advances in body armor, surgical practice, and evacuation methods, more soldiers will survive combat. However, some have lost limbs, sustained burns, or suffered internal injuries that may not be visible to others. This may be new to your employee population, but it should be handled like any other disability issue. Raising awareness among staff of how to acknowledge disabilities can be extremely helpful. Above all, it is important to recognize that veterans as a group are accustomed to being active and want to be active in spite of sustained injuries. It is not uncommon for an injured veteran to have an admirably positive attitude and sense of pride relative to his or her disability.

Closing Thoughts

By viewing veterans in the civilian workplace as a diversity matter, organizations can anticipate challenges, mitigate risk, differentiate between a performance issue and a transition issue, and intervene effectively. Employers may consider flexible schedules to accommodate appointments. The alternative is a group of promising talent, accustomed to performing at or above expected standards, struggling to acclimate. In the process, satisfaction and retention suffer, and nothing is done to bridge the gap of understanding between military and civilian worlds.

A word of caution lest you feel overwhelmed by all that needs to be done to welcome and retain veterans into your organization: don't be paralyzed from doing *something* by a desire to do *everything*. Simple things can have great impact. For example: You know you've got a

FIGURE 4.3

Putting It All Together
Quick Inventory

What is my company doing to support injured veterans/
wounded warriors in the workplace?
1. _____
2. _____
3. _____

What ideas do I have to improve what we can do to support
injured veterans in the workplace?
1. _____
2. _____
3. _____

veteran coming in for his first day of work. You happen to know of another veteran somewhere else in the organization. You ask that veteran to be the new hire's learning buddy for the first two weeks of employment—to let the new hire shadow, ask questions, be an available resource. Essentially, you are enabling peer mentorship based on trust that will automatically emerge between two veterans, even if they don't know each other, which leads us back to the original discussion of veterans as a diverse community within the broader employee community.

What It Means for Us

From my blog post of April 13, 2010

This morning I gave a presentation titled "Employing America's Heroes: What HR Professionals Need to Know About Veterans" to the Baltimore Industry Liaison Group. Lots of good discussion and questions. From there I fled to catch a train to New York, where I am attending the annual conference of *Human Resource Executive Magazine.*

After checking into the hotel, I proceeded to the wrong bank of elevators and rode it for awhile before realizing my mistake and getting off. Waiting with me for the next car down was a young guy—early twenties at most—with one arm covered in tattoos and the other arm gone. Beside him was a canvas tote bag with a large prosthetic arm sticking out. He was not in uniform; rather, he wore a plain T-shirt, jeans, and a baseball cap. I wanted to acknowledge him but hesitated, thinking, "This has to be a war injury. But . . . what if it isn't? No, it has to be—why else would a twenty-something have such an injury?" Before opening my mouth to ask him about it, he asked me a question. "Ma'am, do you know if you have to turn in your room key?" I said I wasn't sure but didn't think so. I asked him if he had served, and when he said yes, I thanked him. He replied, "Oh, thank you, ma'am. It was my pleasure and I served with a smile."

He took his room key out of his pocket and said, "I hate walking through the lobby with this prosthetic arm, getting stared at." I said, "Let me do it. It's the least I can do." He seemed relieved. I felt humbled.

As I walked to the front desk with his key, I thought to myself, "This is what it is going to mean for us." "Us," meaning us Americans. Civilians. Going about our daily lives, we may encounter someone with a visible war injury. My friends who work in the Department of Defense's Wounded Warrior program have said that wounded veterans don't want pity from civilian employers and coworkers, but a little patience is helpful. "Soldiers are used to being active and they want to be active again, even if they are injured. They will be active again."

For those of us civilians who have only experienced war through the media . . . where we might want to look away, we need to look ahead. Where we want to be silent, we need to say thank you. It is only our own discomfort that stands in the way. My encounter today with the young serviceman who had lost his arm showed me a bit about what the war meant for him. Bearing witness to the returning injured and welcoming them home is what it means for us. (For more on Wounded Warriors, see Chapter 10.)

Conclusion to Part 1

THE OBJECTIVE OF PART 1 was to give you a broad perspective on the topic of veterans entering the civilian workplace, what you as a manager or HR professional can expect to see in this segment of the market for talent. We can now look specifically at the military transition experience (Part 2) and how you can impact success and retention throughout the employee lifecycle (Part 3).

Hopefully you received a lot of information and insight in Part 1 regarding key differences between military service and civilian employment. You now have an edge over your competitors who lack this information. Why? Remember the goals of the book. Having read part 1, you are already better prepared to (1) anticipate and head off challenges related to the military-to-civilian transition, (2) gain maximum leverage from the strengths brought by military service members, and (3) position service members for success in your organization.

Part 1 has given you material for developing a business case for hiring veterans and for considering them in your organization's diversity and inclusion programs. The great thing about common challenges is that you can apply a group solution rather than dealing with the same problems over and over with each individual. This perspective can make you a hero in your organization because it leads to economical approaches to retaining valued military hires, which improves organizational ROI.

Part 2

Understanding Military Transition

CHAPTER 5

The Military Transition Framework™

"WOW, I DIDN'T THINK IT was going to be this different."

The most basic aspect of the military-to-civilian transition is that it represents a significant life change. It affects almost every aspect of life (e.g., family, community, daily routines), as opposed to the transition from one civilian job to another, which centers mostly on work and job performance. Even if a service member has prior experience managing civilians in a military context, it does not equate to working with them in a nonmilitary setting. I have consistently found that former service members who truly recognize the magnitude of this change have smoother transitions down the line.

Why is the magnitude of this change difficult to recognize? Because, to date, transition programs offered by the military prior to separation have not focused on preparing service members for civilian employment. Instead, these programs focus on preparing them for the civilian job-search process (e.g., resume preparation, job search tips). This makes a certain amount of sense. However, as a result, veterans are often shocked by how different everything is in the civilian work environment. Many have told us that the hardest part of the military transition is grasping the concept that "you don't know what you don't know."

A 2010 survey of former service members in the first five years of civilian employment asked how different military service was from civilian employment. Sixty percent responded "completely different," while 40 percent responded "moderately different." Note that no one said it was any more similar than that. Respondents identified six key factors that distinguished civilian employment from military service:

1. Lack of leadership
2. Lack of accountability
3. Lack of focus
4. Lack of integrity
5. Lack of motivation
6. Emphasis on profit

What stands out for you in these responses?

Think back to Chapter 2 on organizational culture. Because military culture is so strong and is likely the only professional experience its members have known, other organizational cultures often seem different and, to the veteran, wrong in comparison. This is why your ability to anticipate challenges and calibrate expectations during onboarding is so important; you'll have an easier time helping veterans acclimate to your organization if they know what to expect.

It reminds me of the old adage that if all you have is a hammer, everything looks like a nail. I see three possible courses of action in this case: (1) contort everything into the shape of a nail so you can use your hammer to deal with it, (2) dismiss as unfit anything that can't be repurposed into a nail, or (3) recognize that it is *you* that has the limitation, not the nail (or the hammer, for that matter), which is just being a nail.

I wonder how the adage would be different if it went like this: "If all you have is a hammer, everything looks like a nail. But most things are not a nail, so your hammer will only get you so far, after which point it will utterly fail you. So you'd better get yourself some additional tools." In this scenario, you—the civilian line manager or HR professional—are the owner of the hardware store. The more tools you have in stock to generously offer the customer, the better off you will both be as a result. Lest I portray the service member as unreasonably high-maintenance, keep in mind that *any* new employee coming to you from another strong organizational culture will need some help updating his or her toolbox.

After many years of working with veterans in civilian organizations, I began to observe consistent patterns. I saw three distinct stages, which I labeled detaching, regrouping, and integrating. Individuals who transitioned smoothly into civilian success seemed to progress through the stages fairly quickly. Individuals who struggled with the transition—letting go of the military way of working and adopting the civilian way of working—seemed to get stuck in one or both of the first two stages. After testing my hypotheses, I developed a model to illustrate the process, now known as the Military Transition Framework,™ or MTF. (See Figure 5.1 on the next page.)

(1) Detaching is internally focused and has to do with the identity shift that needs to occur for a veteran to be successful in civilian employment. Detaching is characterized by a mix of feelings, thoughts, and behavior changes. Detaching requires one to mentally and emotionally step away from the defined lifestyle of the military.

(2) Regrouping is externally focused and has to do with interacting with people and work in a civilian context. It can be a lengthy stage of the Framework because it encompasses so much learning. Even if a veteran receives new-hire orientation to acquaint him or her with the new organization, there are overarching aspects of civilian work that need to be covered as well. Regrouping is the process of learning how to operate in a civilian environment and to effectively apply the knowledge, skills, and abilities acquired through military service.

FIGURE 5.1

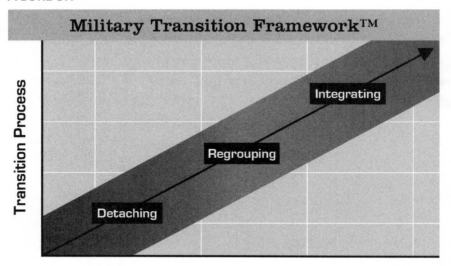

Note that the military transition assistance programs do not teach service members to detach or regroup. If you are a service member's first civilian employer, you as line or HR manager will need to spend time helping the military new-hire regroup into *your* workplace . . . if you want to accelerate the learning process, reduce error, and build and position the veteran for success.

(3) Integrating is the destination of the transition journey, and it occurs both internally to the individual and externally in his or her observable behavior. You'll know that veterans have achieved this phase of transition when you see them smoothly adapting to new ways of doing things with a sense of having integrated a new way of operating and, for many, a new way of being. They will know they've integrated when they can effectively apply their skills and experience in a way that adds value to the civilian organization and brings a feeling of satisfaction and belonging.

Something to keep in mind is that you don't know where in the transition process any given new-hire will be when he or she joins your organization. And while you can certainly say that a long career of military service means that the military way of doing things is more entrenched, you can also say that regardless of length of military service, it is probably the only professional experience the individual has had. The person doesn't know anything other than the military. And, as I've said (and as they have said to me), "they don't know what they don't know." It is to your retention advantage to debunk assumptions early on in the cultural assimilation process.

Your ability to be a mentor and coach—while respecting the individual's career experience and knowledge—can be invaluable as a feedback mechanism. Initially, the service member may not be attuned to how people are responding to him or her, even in a nuanced way, and may not see that anything needs to change. Specifically, the military is so much more straightforward and without subtext. You'll want to avoid the assumption that such military hires are willfully resisting change. Assume the opposite: give benefit of the doubt when there is a question mark as to intention because nine times out of ten missteps are completely out of the person's awareness. Clarify the expectations of *your* particular workplace. In addition, if you can define the intent—the "why"—of success and what it looks like even in a chaotic and rapidly changing environment, it will enable the individual new-hire to take initiative, feel ownership, and provide feedback and suggestions for best practices. This is practical guidance for use with any and all new-hires, but especially with those coming to you from the military.

The following chapters in this section detail each of these three stages and how you can use the Military Transition Framework™ to support the early success and ultimate retention of your military hires.

FIGURE 5.2

Military Transition Assistance and Civilian Transition Assistance

Two Essential Pieces of the Transition Puzzle

Military transition assistance programs provide tactical training to service members preparing to enter the civilian job market	Civilian transition assistance programs provide strategic support to veterans, focused on success in the civilian workplace
Basic resume & cover letter preparation	Cultural differences between the military and civilian workplace
Job hunting tips	The impact of military transition on identity
Job interview skills	Civilian operating procedures
Job fairs with local, regional, and national employers	Cultural acclimation: Tips for civilian success
Connections with military networking groups	Cultural acclimation: Pitfalls to avoid

Military transition assistance programs are available to all separating service members. Civilian transition assistance programs are made available to veterans by a small but growing number of civilian organizations who hire them.

CHAPTER 6

Detaching

"My whole life had been defined by the military. [Transition is] a whole change process and I think a lot of people just take off the uniform on Friday and go back to work on Monday for a government job or contractor and they never really take the time to go through that process. To be open to the change and understand that you may have been hired because of what you know from the military, is not what's going to keep you successful."

—OFFICER, U.S. ARMY[1]

"DETACH" IS A COMMON WORD that can have multiple meanings depending on the context in which it is used. In the context of military transition, I define it as a verb, meaning to mentally step away from the defined lifestyle of the military. Detaching is an internal process characterized by a mix of feelings, thoughts, and behavior changes.

In some ways it is easiest to recognize detaching by its absence. There is a commonly used expression to describe the individual who has not detached from the military; it is said that he or she needs to "take off the uniform." Even though this is a metaphor, it can also be interpreted literally in terms of the actual physical uniform. The service member has traded a long-worn uniform for civilian garb. He or she is the same person as before, but military accomplishments and hard-earned status are suddenly invisible without the uniform.

> "When you transition into the civilian world, you do have to prove yourself all over again. You're very much an unknown commodity to the civilian world. They know—certainly the employers recognize that you did something—you did well in the military, you did good things; but you're just one of the workforce now and that loss of prestige, I think, is hard for some officers to deal with after literally spending an entire lifetime's career achieving and then enjoying it."
>
> —OFFICER, USAF[2]

Individuals who are still in uniform, so to speak, after their formal separation from the military have some consistent behaviors. For example, they may cope with the ambiguity of a personnel policy by imposing structure and limits on things that shouldn't be structured or limited, and unwittingly damage employee morale. Or they may insist on doing things the military way even if it creates stress for themselves and others. It is not unusual to hear an overuse of openers such as, "When I was in the military" or "That's not how it's done on my watch," which demonstrate a resistance to other, nonmilitary ways of doing things.

> "A trap that military guys can fall into is to say, 'I used to be somebody, and let me tell you all the cool things I did.' So there's a certain need to win acceptance because people just look right past you. They don't even know you used to be somebody. You're just some guy. So that can fire up an urge to overtell about your experience. What I found useful was the less I said about the Marine Corps, the better off I was. And the best way I found to refer to previous experience was to simply say, 'In a previous life I once

had this experience that I did this,' and I always described it func-
tionally."

—Officer, USMC[3]

The Challenge of Detaching

The number one goal of Detaching is to constructively separate from
the previous identity as a military service member, to "take off the
uniform." This is directly related to success as a civilian professional
because it is a necessary precursor to integrating. "Taking off the uniform" is not only an essential part of the transition process, but it is
often the most difficult. For the duration of one's military career, the
uniform was a clear and undeniable symbol of identity. By design, the
uniform signaled to others how to address one another and kept a
vast number of personnel organized and focused on the military's mission. The most common feeling experienced to some degree, especially
by those with ten or more years of service, is a sense of loss. This is a
natural response to the transition that seems to linger with time if left
unaddressed.

> "When you get out, it's kind of like a shock to the system. . . . It
> took a long time to find my place, my niche. It was very tough
> after being in a job where you're the top guy and you know what
> you're doing and people seek you out as the expert, for your opin-
> ions."
>
> —Enlisted Service Member, USAF[4]

You may be wondering how this can be the case given that career
military personnel are used to integrating into new cultures and duty
stations every few years. In fact, many service members consider this
part of the joy of service. They pride themselves on their ability to drop
into a new environment and be immediately effective. Many describe a
change of duty station as both seamless—thanks to the military infrastructure—and exciting. So in essence, all else being equal, it's a rela-

tively smooth transition. Understandably, many long-term service members expect the transition to civilian employment to be like a change of duty station, but it's not. Far from it. In civilian organizations, all else is *not* equal. Not even close. It's unlike any previous career move they have made. Think about it this way: The military, it's not just a job, it's an identity. Again: taking off the uniform.

Civilian organizations generally can't lay claim to employee identity because their employees come and go every day, and think of their jobs as just one aspect of life. They don't live on a base where they work, where their kids go to school, where they work with their neighbors. Service members have been living in a family-oriented community that's connected by a set of shared values and protocols of behavior, in which home life and work life are closely aligned and mutually supportive.

> "In the military, even those who only sign up for three or four years kind of throw themselves into it. I had never encountered people who worked to live, not lived to work. It was a bit of a shockaroo to me that a person could actually make a life choice that 'I'm going to make a paycheck to support the thing that matters to me . . . which is not here.'"
>
> —Officer, USMC[5]

Detaching is a very personal process of defining self differently, and it is important to know and accept it as a process . . . NOT a deliverable.

To Take Off the Uniform, You Have to Tone Down the DRUMS First

The military is notorious for its use of acronyms, so in that spirit I coined the acronym DRUMS to illustrate the challenge of Detach. It stands for Default Reaction: Use Military Style. Under stress or uncertainty, most of us fall back on what we're accustomed to—our comfort zone. For a service member, this "default" reaction will be to use what worked in the military, also known as "command and control." By definition, DRUMS drown out everything else around them. DRUMS can sound very strong, aggressive, and directive in a way that feels heavy-handed in some civilian situations. DRUMS can be damaging to work relationships, creating barriers between people. DRUMS can create resistance to working together and to learning.

> "I worked with a career officer who had a hard time adapting to civilian culture. When he would meet resistance his behavior pattern would revert to even more of the military behavior that allowed him to succeed there, which, of course further exacerbated the situation. He developed a reputation as someone who wasn't able to think creatively, who viewed life and the business world as checklist-oriented, and someone who would growl at you. This created problems in his civilian peer group and with his staff."
>
> —Officer, USAF[6]

In order to tone down the DRUMS, the service member must acknowledge that there is more than one legitimate way to accomplish something, ways other than the military way. This again goes to setting early expectations with new-hire veterans so they understand from the earliest days that not only will different approaches be used in the civilian environment, but that to use a military approach would actually do damage and create problems. With your patience and supportive feedback, the veteran will eventually put down—or at least tone down—his or her DRUMS in exchange for attitudes and behaviors more consistent with civilian success.

Coaching Conversations Can Help

Assisting former service members with Detaching is surprisingly simple. As a trained and certified leadership coach, I know firsthand the powerful impact of listening and validating the experience of a transitioning veteran. Listening without judgment, listening to learn and understand, is a gift to the speaker and something many have never experienced. The following is an example of what I would call a "coaching conversation," but which can be initiated by you or anyone who wants to help veterans transition.

Coaching Conversation: Transition Process

Emily: Carol, you're wrapping up your first week with us. How's it going?

Carol: Oh, it's a whirlwind, but very positive. I can't wait to dig in and contribute.

Emily: I know it can be frustrating to figure out how to do your job in a new environment.

Carol: Yes, I keep calling my manager "Sir," and he keeps correcting me!

Emily: What has it been like for you, leaving military service?

Carol: Oh, every day is an adventure—I never know what's coming. It seems I've lost all my familiar daily routines. Kind of disorienting!

Emily: Routines are comforting! What routines would you like to integrate into your civilian life?

Carol: I think getting home in time to have dinner with my family would be helpful for all of us—we are all acclimating to the fluctuating work schedule and haven't crossed paths too much this week.

Emily: That does sound important. Is there anything I can do to help make that happen?

Carol: Well, I guess it would be good to know if leaving at 5 p.m. is acceptable or frowned upon . . . I notice a lot of cars in the office parking lot long after dark!

Emily: I know what you mean, and I think each person has to make his or her own choices about that kind of thing. What has surprised you the most about leaving military service?

Carol: Definitely the loss of camaraderie. I'm used to having my friends around me when I work, seeing neighbors at the commissary, going to events at my kids' school on base. Now everything feels kind of disconnected.

Emily: That sounds like a big adjustment. How are you coping with it?

Carol: Initially, it was kind of a letdown . . . I was excited about leaving the military and starting my new life, but then it felt like the rug was pulled out from under me. At least when I changed jobs and duty stations in the military, it was still the military and a lot remained the same from place to place. Things just got taken care of for you. Now, nothing gets done unless I do it myself!

Emily: I imagine that could be overwhelming. I know from working with other veterans over the years that it all takes time to get used to, and pacing yourself can help a lot. I know someone in the finance department who left service about a year ago and faced some of the same challenges you're describing. I'd like to introduce you to each other so you can benefit from what he learned along the way. Would you be interested in that?

Carol: Yes! That would be great! It is always quicker to learn from someone else's mistakes than to make them all yourself!

Successful Detaching

Plenty of service members are excited about life outside the military and can't wait to dive into the choices and freedoms they'll have as civilians. I have observed that individuals who served in the military for shorter terms, less than ten years for example, seem more enthusiastic and less trepidatious about the transition to civilian employment. My explanation is simple: the more time spent in the military (or any strong culture), the more deeply ingrained it is in the individual, the more it is their "first nature." In contrast, service members who leave the military after three to five years, for example, are younger with less work experience and are therefore less entrenched in the military way of doing things. (An exception to be sensitive to is the 18–24 year old who does not choose to leave service but is medically discharged due to combat injury. This individual may experience Detaching differently as a result of the circumstances surrounding separation from service.)

Service members who approach civilian employment with a positive and enthusiastic posture tend to move quickly through the detaching stage because they aren't resisting change. These individuals often come across as being:

- Open to whatever the world may present them with
- Humble about the fact that they are newbies when it comes to being civilians
- Successful earlier in their civilian careers because they can adapt quickly
- Receptive to civilian culture and operations

You, as an HR or line manager, can assist with the Detaching process by coaching veterans to use a few proven techniques:

- Observe external cues.
- Think forward, not backward.
- Reword directives into requests.
- Acknowledge the magnitude of change that goes along with leaving the military.

- Accept the ambiguity that goes along with starting something new (in this case, starting to *not* be in the military anymore).
- Take time to discover and explore who they are or want to be without the uniform.

Moving through detaching makes life so much easier than resisting it. It actually allows the individual to learn differently because the mental filters are open, not shut down the way they are in resistance.

Closing Thoughts

You don't have to be a coach or counselor to make a difference in someone's Detaching process. Start by being curious. Avoid fixing and problem solving. When it comes to the emotional side of military transition, being able to talk about the experience goes a long way toward working through it. Chances are good the veteran can solve his or her own problems—in fact, it is probably a strength. The unique value you can add to the Detaching process is to simply acknowledge its validity and let the veteran know he or she has your support.

CHAPTER 7

Regrouping

REGROUPING CAN BEGIN during the veteran's job-search process and end when he or she has adopted a new way of operating that is consistent with civilian success. Unlike Detaching, which is an internal identity-related process, Regrouping is an external behavior-related process in which the veteran is continually confronted with new ways of doing things and approaches that conflict with military practice. Hallmarks of this stage of transition are a steep learning curve, resistance to change, receiving and responding to feedback, and, ultimately, sustained behavior change. You, as leader, manager, and/or human resource professional are in a position to accelerate the learning curve and limit frustration.

The Challenge of Regrouping

Regrouping does not necessarily begin after detaching has been completed. The two stages are not dependent upon each other that way. Regrouping begins when the service member is first faced with the unfamiliar world of civilian employment. This may be during the job-search process when he or she starts to experience how different a civilian organization is from the military in terms of language, priorities, values, and organization cultures. Regrouping comes into full force as the new-hire engages with his or her new employer.

As you can imagine, adopting new ways of thinking, doing, and being is more easily done when one is not resisting change. Resistance to new approaches and attachment to military approaches is a primary indicator that an individual is still working through the Detaching stage. Ideally, the individual is well into the Detaching process before starting a new job, but "ideal" is the operative word here, as it rarely happens that way. When possible, I advise service members to take a breather of a month or two, or three, or even six, to allow Detaching to happen naturally. However, this is unrealistic for many who depend upon the steady paycheck of the military.

Several of my clients who were general officers took advantage of the opportunity to step back and consider their next move, and each and every one of them testifies to the benefit of having taken time off. They tell me it made their transition into civilian employment smoother because they had had time to mentally "take off the uniform" and consider who they might be without it. This period of reflection allowed them to make thoughtful choices about employment rather than jumping at the first opportunity that came their way, which increased the likelihood of a good fit. Detaching can be a period of great personal growth.

The biggest challenge of Regrouping is trying to do it while fully immersed in the Detaching process. Regrouping can be fraught with frustration, interpersonal missteps, unnecessary anxiety, and resistance to the new reality. This is challenging to the individual as well as to those at the receiving end. Those who might genuinely try to help the service member succeed find it frustrating to stand by and watch the individual get in his or her own way time and time again until they either quit or experience a significant mental shift.

Veterans themselves say it best, so let's look at Regrouping through the eyes of some veterans kind enough to share what it was like for them:

> "Most of the disciplines learned in the military aren't perceived the same in the civilian world, so I had to adapt. Conforming to the civilian's version of what's accepted, preferred and frowned upon was frustrating because it caused me to be 'tripped up,' although it was unintentional."
>
> —ENLISTED SERVICE MEMBER, US COAST GUARD[1]

> "[The civilian world] seemed confusing and chaotic for me coming out of the service, while things were more organized and defined in the military. In the service I felt I had people willing to instruct me and it was more direct on the success and failure side. 'Do these tasks and you will be successful.' In civilian life it is, 'You do these tasks and if we like your style or personality, you will be successful.'"
>
> —ENLISTED SERVICE MEMBER, US NAVY[2]

> "I was given a task as soon as I started working and I was expected to complete it with only a minimal amount of knowledge of how. . . . So I had to ask a lot of questions and depend on other personnel to help me accomplish the task rather than be able to find a reference or manual to read and direct me. That made me feel kind of inadequate even though I had completed twenty-four years in the Marine Corps and I was, at one time, the go-to person on getting things done. I felt very small. In the Marine Corps you have a Directive on almost every subject, so that was a little difficult to get used to."
>
> —ENLISTED SERVICE MEMBER, USMC[3]

In part 1, we discussed the many cultural differences that can make military transition challenging. Those all come to life in Regrouping. For example, learning about communication and decision-making styles, the role of organizational mission, and what it means to lead a voluntary workforce—this is the learning of the Regrouping stage.

> "In the military, particularly once you gain rank, people assume that you're kind of right. And so, even though you want to get everybody's perspective, people put more stock and value in whatever you say and generally go in that direction. I found on the civilian side, you get a lot more done if you get people collaborating, get everybody's input, and go forward from there. It may not be the right solution. I guess it's more important to make some progress for all concerned than it is to be right. My experience working with civilians says it's more important to get everybody to buy into a solution even though it might not be your version of the right solution. You'll make much more progress by getting everybody involved."
>
> —OFFICER, US ARMY[4]

At its essence, the challenge of Regrouping is finding the right balance of focus on task (mission) and focus on relationship. To master civilian culture, it is imperative that one understands the nature of tasks and relationships because the two exist in parallel. What do I mean by this? In the military, when a direct order is given it is carried out as part of the standard operating procedure. Because the civilian mission is different, its workplace is less structured and *relationships replace protocol as the way to get things done*. In civilian life, no one is compelled to follow orders to the letter or on a specific time frame. Certainly direct reports should and generally do care about performing well against the boss's standards, but what about the boss's peers and other colleagues? They have their own priorities. So it is easier and quicker to get things done if the person you are requesting help from knows and feels favorably toward you.

> "Sometimes you've got to look at your long-term relationships and not just being so mission-focused. That was a big light bulb

for me and so I do act differently within my organization and actually think a little bit differently because of that. . . . It definitely has gotten better. My colleagues are more receptive to me personally because of this attitude change in how I approach and listen to people. It also has helped me to get some perspective that I normally would have just discounted. Now my perspective is much wider that I'm going to listen to everybody's opinions."

—Officer, USAF[5]

In any given interaction, regardless of urgency, there is room to promote or damage the connection with others. As we all know, trust takes a long time to build and about a millisecond to break.

This concept is illustrated nicely by the e-mail exchange below, between Al and Tom, taken from actual transcripts.

FIGURE 7.1

E-Mail Exchange

From: Al (civilian peer) **Date/Time:** Sept. 8th, 11:00am
To: Tom (former Army Lt. Col)
Subject: Presentation slides

Good morning Tom: Some of my staff over here in the Systems team attended yesterday's symposium and heard your presentation. I'd like to take you up on the offer to get the slides in soft copy, since the topic relates to the work we're doing. The slides will be a good resource for the team going forward.

Thanks and I look forward to hearing from you,
Al

From: Tom **Date/Time:** Sept. 8th, 11:05am
To: Al
Subject: Presentation slides

Give me some times you're available
r/
Tom

2:30p.m.: Al returns to his desk after several meetings, and begins reading through the fifteen e-mail messages awaiting him. He comes to Tom's response and has no clue what it means. He asks himself, "What does my availability have to do with sending the slides over e-mail?" Al looks back at his sent message to remind himself of the context.

Still puzzled, he sends this reply:

From: Al	**Date/Time:** Sept. 8th, 2:35pm
To: Tom	
Subject: RE: Presentation slides	

Tom, are you asking what time I'd be available to pick them up? I was hoping you could just e-mail the document.
Thanks, Al
p.s. What is "r/"?

From: Tom	**Date/Time:** Sept. 8th, 2:37pm
To: Al	
Subject: Presentation slides	

Assuming you want to go over the presentation

Al reads this and thinks, "What's with the cryptic answers? Could this guy make it any harder to get this done? Forget it; I don't have time to go back and forth on this." Al walks away from the exchange with a feeling of exasperation and annoyance with Tom.

Closing Thoughts

Successful regrouping means an individual has toned down the DRUMS enough to hear and see what's happening outside of him or herself and modify behavior based on external clues about the new environment. I have seen a set of characteristics common to service members who have moved through the regrouping stage. They:

- Have a healthy respect for the unknown and err on the side of caution vs. assumption.
- Feel energized by their own new ideas and those of others, including staff.

- Welcome new experiences and an alternative way of doing things.
- Are flexible in interpreting rules.
- Fully bring their skill and experience to bear . . . while remaining humble about what they do not know or understand.
- Are willing to roll up their sleeves and be "doers" when necessary.
- And . . . continually practice the skills of listening, observing, and inquiring to (1) get valuable information and (2) adopt an interpersonal style different from that of the military.

The military is all about training for things that might or might not happen, and executing on immediate requirements. Therefore, service members are accustomed to being in learning mode, to practicing, honing, and drilling their skills. They describe themselves as highly trainable, eager to learn, improve, and grow. It is a vital part of the military culture. Civilian organizations can and should take advantage of it.

Part 3, the Veteran Retention Lifecycle, will get into the details of regrouping and how to accelerate the learning curve.

FIGURE 7.2

Putting It All Together
Monday Morning Quarterback

What went awry in the e-mail exchange between Al and Tom? As an objective third party, how would you explain it?

_____

_____

_____

_____

How would you advise Al to enable a more productive exchange with Tom in the future?

_____

_____

_____

_____

How would you advise Tom to enable a more productive exchange with Al in the future?

_____

_____

_____

_____

What are some things you could say or do to prevent this initial disconnect from occurring between veterans and civilians in the future?

_____

_____

_____

_____

FIGURE 7.3

Before and After Regrouping

Before Regrouping	After Regrouping
1. "Oh, I've done this before. The best way to do it is this way. . ."	1. "I've done something like this in another context and I wonder if it would work here."
2. "I keep telling them exactly what's going to happen if they do it that way, but no one wants to hear it."	2. "The team needs to feel a sense of ownership for this to work, so we're exploring the options together for now."
3. "I don't know why they left me out of the loop on this, since it is why they hired me."	3. "This looks like an oversight . . . I'll offer my insight and see if they take me up on it."
4. "I'm just waiting for one of my buddies to get me into his company."	4. "At first I thought this place was nuts, but it didn't take long to see that I was the one that needed to adjust. Glad I realized it when I did!"

Leadership: Filling In the Blanks

By Emily King, adapted from
www.mymilitarytransition.com/blog post of:
June 24, 2009

The topic of leadership is front and center in most professional settings, certainly in the military and business worlds. Both have devoted themselves to the practice of leadership, contributing to the culture's understanding of what it means to lead. But despite agreement on this point, I am struck by the number of problems I see caused by assumptions about the meaning of the word leadership.

To put it simply, military leaders have a value in the civilian market based on extensive leadership experience but often struggle to find a good culture fit in civilian organizations, and at the same time the civilian world struggles to maintain a pipeline of strong leaders. In other words, each group needs what the other has to offer. Here's the rub: when they find each other, opportunity can be lost in translation.

Officers tell me that civilian organizations lack leadership. Organizations hire them for their military leadership experience but then won't allow them to lead, an understandable complaint.

Organizations, on the other hand, tell me that they invest a lot of money in retired officers and receive slow return on that investment because their style of leadership often doesn't work in a civilian setting. Also an understandable complaint.

Aligning the expectations of these two stakeholder groups must begin at the most basic level imaginable: the word itself. Leadership. We all know the word, but are we using the same definition? No. It means completely different things in the military and civilian worlds.

Military leadership is trained and expected from day one. It has specific boundaries and activities associated with it, a clear protocol for accomplishing a clear mission, and a heavy strategic component. The organization is designed to build leaders. In contrast, civilian leaders may or may not be trained . . . leadership roles are often earned on the basis of good performance over time, subject matter expertise, or technical prowess. The lack of standardized training, philosophy, and role definition in civilian environments means leadership can look a hundred different ways, most of which are not recognizable as leadership to former military folks.

Understanding this basic reality is essential to calibrating expectations on both sides. Retiring military personnel are best served by refraining from standing in judgment of what they see in the civilian world . . . In other words, rather than observing how ineffective things are, they should observe, with the curiosity of a sociologist, how interesting things are. Viewing civilian operations in the context of civilian goals is key to success.

Likewise, hiring organizations—including government entities—would be best served by looking underneath the label of "leader" to see what it actually means in terms of span of control, decision rights, capacity to influence people and events, etc. Understanding what a retired military officer is bringing to the table in tangible terms is key to fully leveraging him or her and accelerating return on the hiring investment.

Because leadership can be an amorphous concept in the civilian world—not lacking, necessarily, just loosely defined—organizations that hire military officers need to add a layer of rigor to their self-understanding. They must reflect on what leadership means and requires in their particular business model and culture. This last point applies to all civilian organizations, really, not just those that hire retired officers. "You get what you measure," as they say, and you can't measure something until you know how to recognize it.

Civilian organizations exist in a completely different realm from the military because they have to stay competitive/profitable in a constantly changing marketplace. This fact alone creates an imperative for flexible, "agile" structures and methods that can anticipate the subtlest of shifts. Watch the financial segment of any news show and you'll see reports of shares going up and down by the minute. These fluctuations are very real to business leaders.

Bottom line: In my experience, military officers are most successful when they can assess civilian operations and leadership in their proper context, which is not a military context. Civilian organizations, on the other hand, are most successful when they can (1) articulate and support standards of leadership and (2) translate them for incoming military hires.

CHAPTER 8

Integrating

INTEGRATING IS THE THIRD AND FINAL STEP in the Military Transition Framework™. It is the destination of the military transition journey. You will know former service members have completed detaching and regrouping and entered integrating when you see them working *with* the flow (rather than against the flow), smoothly adapting to new ways of doing things. This is most evident when a new service member joins the organization and you think to yourself, "Oh, yes, I remember so-and-so making that mistake when he was new. He would never do that now."

Signposts of Integration

I have seen integration demonstrated in a myriad of ways, sometimes simply by the absence of issues and challenges. Other things to look for include:

- More expansive thinking, free of resistance to nonmilitary interpretations

- No defensiveness about what isn't known or understood
- Capacity to use humor to lighten uncomfortable moments
- Ability to transfer and translate previous experience into valuable assets
- Ability to blend new ways of operating with those that made them successful before
- Ability to establish trust and credibility by embracing the methods of others
- Consistent performance at a high level and stretching professionally
- Genuine enjoyment of the job, colleagues, and new civilian self
- Openness to/excitement about the possibility of a long-term role in the organization

Comments I've heard from veterans who are fully integrated into their civilian environments include things like "I'm really enjoying the freedom I now have to try different approaches. If I have an idea that sounds interesting, I usually get the green light to give it a try. Then we assess afterwards to see how it worked." Or "My first few months out were tough because it was like learning a new language. But I'm getting it now and I feel like I am finally making a contribution." Or "Things aren't always written down in terms of rules of engagement. There have been some awkward learning opportunities but we just laugh about them afterwards."

Integration and Career Management

Integrating doesn't mean the veteran stops learning or never makes another mistake. It means she has let go of absolutes from the military and opened her mind to another way of doing and being. Even when things go wrong, she now has them in perspective and can address them constructively. It is a mindset that says she has taken off the uniform.

In many organizations, integration looks like readiness for promotion or added responsibility. It may not be possible to put a finger on what has shifted in the veteran, but it is enough simply to observe that they now "get it" about working effectively in the environment. There is no timeline for when an individual reaches integration because it is the culmination of internal and external transition, both highly personal processes.

While integration is often viewed by observers as readiness for what's next, it is also the point where a former service member begins to think about career management. This should not be confused with the job hopping that can occur during detaching or regrouping, which is based on dissatisfaction with current employment; rather, career management in the integration stage is about owning one's career and making thoughtful decisions about how to build on success. After all, it is difficult to contemplate success at the next level while one is struggling to be successful at the current level. When the energy spent in the struggle can be directed toward career planning, integration has most likely occurred.

Chances are good the veteran will have career options in your organization he or she never had in the military. The most obvious example that comes to mind is the option to enjoy a successful career in-grade rather than seeking promotion. Every organization is different, but generally an organization needs a stable base of "solid citizen" performers who get the job done well and keep the bus on the road, so to speak.

This points to another cultural difference between the military and some civilian organizations: The military organization is dependent upon a constant cycle of promotion. The emphasis is on preparing each person for his or her next job, which will become available when the person currently in that job moves up to his or her next job. In the words of one officer in the U.S. Army,[1] "In the military, when your boss asks you what your next job is, the appropriate response is, '*Your* job, boss.' Can you imagine saying that to a civilian boss?!"

The military can be said to use an "up or out" model of career development, in which one is expected to progress at a prescribed rate.

If one does not, one leaves the organization. The option of remaining at a junior rank simply does not exist as it does in many civilian organizations. Many of the veterans I have had the pleasure to work with over the years were delighted by the prospect of working a job they enjoy and do well, on a regular schedule, without the mandate to climb a career ladder. Especially after a career of twenty or more years in the military, many want to replace the twenty-four/seven lifestyle with a balance of work and personal activities.

For those who may have aspirations for promotion or increased responsibility, integration is a critical point of contact for you as the manager or HR professional. Why? Because while service members may feel ready, unless they understand available options, they are at risk of looking elsewhere for career opportunities. We will talk about this in greater depth when we get to Chapter 13.

Integration and Developing Others

The spirit of service runs deep in service members, and they love to help more than any other group with which I've worked. If they can smooth the transition of fellow veterans entering the civilian workforce, they are often eager to do so. Integration is the best time to engage them as mentors or learning buddies for military new-hires. Having completed the detaching and regrouping stages of the transition, these employees have the wisdom of experience and the scratches (but not scars) to go with it, and they have a great success story to tell your new-hires. Invite them to help out one-to-one or with groups of new-hires. (Experience with wounded warriors, in particular, is showing the essential role of workplace community for veterans in terms of retention.)

There is another key role integrated veterans can play in your organization in support of their fellows coming in: the role of subject matter expert (SME) when it comes to successful military-to-civilian transition. We'll talk about this at length in Chapter 12, but for now suffice it to say that your program to hire and retain veterans will be well served by the insight and experience of those who have success-fully integrated into your organization.

Closing Thoughts

You can't promise your new-hire service members when they'll feel 100 percent or when they'll be considered for promotion, but you can as-sure them that it can and will happen, and you can provide examples of the signposts I've listed above. Your capacity to be patient with the process and show faith in the individual will go a long way toward accelerating the transition into integration.

Creating opportunities for integrated veterans to support the tran-sition success of other military new-hires is a win-win for all con-cerned, serving to strengthen the bond of employees with your organization. Don't be afraid to ask your integrated veterans for help—my experience is that they will be both happy and proud to oblige!

Conclusion to Part 2

THE OBJECTIVE OF PART 2 was to introduce you to the Military Transition Framework™ (MTF), an important tool for you as manager or HR professional, and provide hands-on guidance for using it with your military new hires.

Think about the Military Transition Framework™ as it pertains to the goals of this book. Simply understanding the complexities of the transition in terms of the three stages of detaching, regrouping, and integrating enables you to *anticipate and head off challenges related to the military-to-civilian transition*. Doing what you can to provide context and guidance in the regrouping stage will enable you to *gain maximum leverage from the strengths brought by military service members*. And, finally, partnering with them to chart a career path in your organization *positions them for success*—long-term success and employment.

An overarching benefit of the MTF is that it normalizes the transition experience for the service member and for your organization. To normalize something is to put it in the broader context of others who have gone before. Normalizing the transition by putting a model around it makes it easy to explain and use as a practical tool, and it lets the service member know that whatever challenges he or she may face now or in the future are just that: normal. Military transition can feel like being a fish out of water, and the MTF clearly illustrates how the experience is shared by all. Knowing that your struggles are "normal" takes the edge off of feeling incompetent in the early days, weeks, and months of civilian employment.

Our next step is to get up close and personal with the everyday, practical applications of the knowledge and insight you've gained up to this point. Onward!

Part 3

The Veteran Retention Lifecycle™

CHAPTER 9

The Veteran Retention Lifecycle™

BEFORE STRIKING OUT ON MY OWN as an independent organization development consultant and executive coach, I had the opportunity to spend five years doing internal "people strategy" for a large consulting firm. People strategy refers to anything and everything pertaining to where the company's business intersects with the people employed by the business. For example, our small but mighty team of four consultants (two behavioral scientists and two MBAs) would be presented with a business problem that had a "people" component, and we would figure out the best solution for both. It was an exciting time, and the team was able to have great impact across the company because we were filling a need no one had previously identified and coming up with innovative business strategies along the way.

Our little consulting group resided ten thousand feet up from the HR organization, like an umbrella under which sat HR, recruiting, training, diversity, compensation and benefits, rewards, etc. From that point of view, we looked at how the moving parts worked, intersected, and blocked one another. In every case, our best solution cut across all the people functions. As a result, each function was forced out of its stovepipe and made to look holistically at business impacts. Initially, the groups and systems worked together reluctantly and reminded me of herding cats. Lots and lots of scratches in the process!

Before too long, however, I came to see the integration process differently. There seemed to be an innate sense of order that I needed to work within. That order is what you may know as the "employee lifecycle." In a lifecycle, things occur in a logical sequence, with room for overlap. This was a useful organizing principle that I continue to use today and that bears well on the matter of military transition. It looks like this now:

In the lifecycle model, every business problem had at least four pieces to figure out: how could we solve the problem without negative impact to *attraction and recruitment*, to *on-boarding and employee engagement*, to *managing performance* over time, to *career opportunities* and, the center-piece: *retention*. Regardless of how straightforward a business problem appeared to be, it ended up impacting every stage of an employee's lifecycle with the organization.

Likewise, while each stage posed potential risks, each stage offered a point of entry for intervening. So it simply required us to turn the question around and ask ourselves, "What would have to change in our attraction and recruitment strategy and process in order to affect the business issue in one direction or another?" and then repeat the question about each stage of the lifecycle. Another way of using the lifecycle was to run down the list and ask:

- What is it about our attraction and recruitment process that con-tributes to or alleviates the business problem at hand?
- What is it about our on-boarding philosophy and approach that contributes to or alleviates the business problem at hand?
- What is it about our performance management process that con-tributes to or alleviates the business problem at hand?
- What is it about our career development tools and processes that contribute to or alleviate the business problem at hand?

FIGURE 9.1

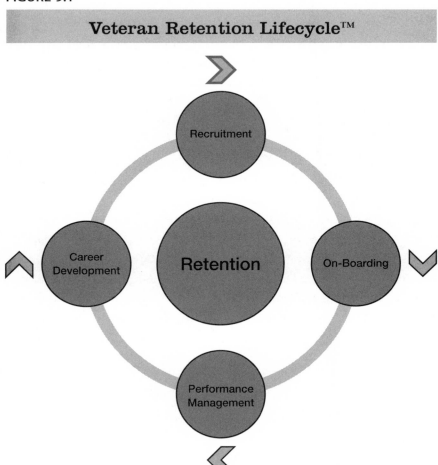

Veteran Retention Lifecycle™

- *What is it about the way these moving parts intersect that alleviates or contributes to the business problem at hand?*

When you've got the root causes identified and it's time to look at solutions, you can look for them in any or all of the four lifecycle stages. How does this apply to veterans transitioning into civilian employment? It applies directly, as you will see in the following five chapters. You will notice that, in this section of the book, I've included some discussion of Wounded Warriors. Many organizations are interested in hiring men and women whose military careers have been cut short by combat injuries. With this interest, however, I have often found questions, concerns, and even resistance, all of which are understandable. My hope is that by addressing the topic head-on, readers will be better informed and prepared to include Wounded Warriors in their hiring strategies.

There is an important exercise called the organizational readiness assessment (ORA) that you can use in part or as a whole to determine where your organization is now and where you'd like it to be, in relation to hiring and retaining veterans (Figure 9-2). I suggest you complete it yourself, based on instinct, and a second time with the help of a cross-functional team made up of someone from Human Resources, Recruitment, Training, Diversity, Benefits, and Organization Development or Effectiveness. Your collective responses to the questions on the ORA will form the structure for any business case you may develop later to gain support for hiring veterans.

FIGURE 9.2

Organizational Readiness Assessment*

In preparing to hire military veterans, you need to first determine if your organization is ready to meet the challenge and take full advantage of these skilled employees. Assemble a cross-functional stakeholder group and engage in honest self-reflection as an organization. Following are high-level categories of questions to consider, along with an example of each. Your answers to the following questions can be the basis of a business case in support of veteran programs.

1. **Rationale and Requirements**
   How serious and/or urgent is this request? Is there commitment among decision makers?

2. **Organizational Context**
   What's happening in the organization now? Where are time and resources being focused?

3. **Organizational Insight**
   What is our previous experience with veterans?

4. **Recruitment**
   Have we ever attempted to recruit from the military? If so, what can we learn from experience?

5. **Engagement and Retention**
   What retention data (quantitative or anecdotal) do we have about those veterans we have hired in the past?

6. **Performance Management**
   How have former military service members performed in our organization?

7. **Career Management**
   Have veterans progressed within our organization? If so, what factors contributed to their success?

8. **Goals and Outcomes**
   What do we want our end-state to look like? How will things be different and how will that help the business?

9. **Measurement and Evaluation**
   How will we know change has occurred? What reference points (performance ratings, retention data, employee engagement surveys) will we use to baseline our current state and measure our progress?

*Source: ASTD InfoLine, "Military to Civilian Onboarding," Vol. 27, Issue 1013, by Emily King. Used with permission from the American Society of Training and Development.

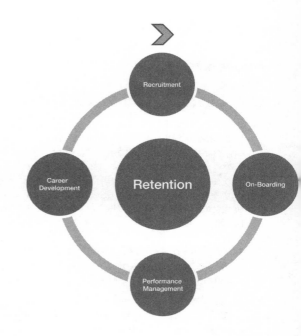

CHAPTER 10

Recruitment

TO RECRUIT MILITARY CANDIDATES to your organization you must offer them a compelling reason to join. This evolves as you implement new programs, but initially all you may have to attract candidates with is a deliberate interest in hiring former service members. Why? Often, the decision comes as a direct result of:

- Market demand
- Positive past experience with veterans
- A broader talent strategy
- An altruistic motivation to support those who have served the nation

Any and all are good reasons to hire veterans. What is the answer to the question of "why" for your organization?

Once you've stated an interest in hiring veterans, the path becomes clear. You simply need to learn how to effectively recruit, hire, on-board, and retain veterans. This chapter will talk about the key steps:

FIGURE 10.1

Attracting Veterans
Consider . . .

What do you offer that is compelling to veterans? Based on your growing insight into them as a community, what would make your organization an attractive employment option?

_____

_____

_____

_____

_____

_____

_____

- Gathering organizational intelligence
- Sourcing candidates
- Interpreting resumes
- Interviewing candidates
- Making the hire

The chapter concludes with a case study that allows you to put all the information together and apply it to a real situation.

Gathering Organizational Intelligence

One sign of effective recruitment is retention. There is no room for growth if an organization's recruiting resources are focused on keeping the revolving door moving with replacement hiring. It is indeed costly to replace employees, especially in an organization whose goal is to grow. So, smart organizations connect the dots between recruiting and retention before they leave the gate, so to speak.

A key aspect of recruiting for retention is understanding the importance of a candidate's "fit" with organizational culture and expectations. In other words, is the person likely to perform and remain engaged over time, given the realities of how things work day to day? Effective recruiters pay some attention to fit by getting to know their organization both in terms of its mission, its business goals, and its personality, if you will. This is helpful when recruiting anyone, not just a former service member. The first section of this book explained how very different the military's organizational personality is from just about any other type of organization. It stands to reason that recruiting for retention might look a little different for former service members. Consider the following questions as a way of recruiting for retention:

How have former service members done in the past, in regard to:

- Cultural integration/fit?
- Time-to-performance (time it takes them to become productive)?
- Sustained performance?
- Career progression?
- Retention?
- Also, do you have a track record to look back on to learn which military hires have been successful and, based on that, what to look for in potential employees?

This is what I mean by gathering intelligence. What it takes to retain a former service member may be unique, and you need to know that before you start recruiting. Unless, that is, you want to spend your time replacing your recruits!

Sounds daunting? It doesn't have to be. There are many ways of gathering intelligence about fit, any one of which is better than nothing. For example, you can:

- Ask around for anecdotal information. Line managers are a great place to start. "Say, do you remember Joe who came to us from the Army a few years back? Why did he decide to leave?" You may need to probe for the small "whys" beneath the big "why." For example, you learn that Joe left because he got a better offer somewhere else. Why was Joe receptive to the offer? Did he find it or did it find him? You may learn that Joe was never really happy in your organization. Why was that? If his manager can't answer this question, I guarantee that that in itself is a useful piece of information. In the military, managers know and stay involved with each and every direct report. No one falls off the radar. Likewise, in successful civilian organizations, managers know and stay involved with employees and every direct report. Remember, people leave managers, not organizations.

- Go to the source by surveying, interviewing, or holding focus groups with key groups:
  - current employees who served in the military
  - former employees who served in the military (if you are permitted to do so)

For example, you might say, "Jane, you have been a successful employee here at Company X for many years. What would you say has contributed to that? What were your initial challenges transitioning here from the Navy? What and who helped you to overcome those challenges? How? What have been your keys to success? How would you advise military new-hires who want to be successful here?"

- Interview internal human resource professionals in your organization and beyond. "In general, do former military service members tend to succeed and stay here? What do you think contributes to their tendency to stay or go? What aspects of our organization's culture or personality help or hinder their success and satisfaction?"

- If your organization permits, conduct exit interviews with all departing employees to identify primary and secondary reasons for terminating, and analyze results in terms of veteran or nonveteran status.

- Be a data hound and query your human resource information system (HRIS). Sample queries:
  - How many past or present employees indicate veteran status?
  - Of this group, what is/was their tenure? Career progression? What are their performance ratings?
  - How do the answers to these questions differ compared to the larger employee population?

Regardless of the method you use to gather intelligence, the information you get as a result may lead you to form hypotheses about the type of veteran you want to look for in the recruiting process. For example, you may see that junior enlisted service members tend to succeed and stay in certain types of jobs or divisions within your organization. That is helpful information. Or you may find that former military officers don't seem to perform as well or stay as long in certain positions as their peers hired from careers in industry.

Chances are that for every hypothesis you make based on the information you gather, many more questions will be raised in the process. The extent to which your organization seeks answers to those questions is the extent to which it will differentiate itself in the market as a veteran-friendly employer of choice. But remember, a little bit of organizational intelligence is better than no organizational intelligence when it comes to recruiting for retention.

Sourcing Candidates

With time, as you and your organization do more and more to welcome and cultivate former service members, you will not have to look for them; they will seek you out. Your goal is to attract top talent through your reputation in the military community as a great place to work.

While you're working toward this goal, however, you may still need to actively source candidates. There's nothing new under the sun when it comes to doing this—you'd pursue military hires in much the same way as you would source any specialized group of candidates:

- Solicit referrals from existing employees with a military background. There's nothing better than word-of-mouth when it comes to reaching candidates who could be a fit with your organization. Reward successful referrals with a monetary reward or token to encourage a steady flow of candidates. This approach has the lowest cost and highest potential return on investment. Further, referrals from a known source may reduce risk of turnover due to lack of fit or unrealistic expectations.
- Post jobs on relevant online sites such as (note: job sites come and go; below are a few we've found to be stable over time):
  - www.vetjobs.com
  - www.esgr.org
  - www.americasheroesatwork.gov
  - www.clearedjobs.net
  - www.gijobs.com
  - www.woundedwarriorproject.org
  - www.military.com
  - www.taonline.com
- Participate in job fairs geared toward service members, such as:
  - http://military.nationalcareerfairs.com
  - www.corporategray.com
  - State and local military career centers
- Host your own job fair
- Connect to organizations chartered to serve veterans and employers, such as:
  - Veteran's Employment and Training Service (dol.gov/vets)
  - Employer Support of the Guard and Reserve (esgr.org)
  - Marine for Life (m4l.usmc.mil)
  - Local military base offices of transition

- Vocational Rehabilitation and Employment Service (vba.gov/bln.vre)
- Advertise in publications geared to past and present service members, such as:
  - *G.I. Jobs*
  - *Military Times*
  - *Military Times Edge*
  - *Stars & Stripes*

Understanding the Military Resume

Have you ever seen the resume of someone who has spent his or her career in the military? It will likely be very different and require a different approach from screeners and recruiters. A bit of context: service members have never had to compile their professional experience in a format we know as a resume. Nor do they have civilian experience or terminology to translate their duties in terms that would be meaningful to the civilian reader. The resume will likely contain unfamiliar acronyms, references, and descriptions that don't readily map to open jobs you're trying to fill. Oh, and the resume may well be four-plus pages in length.

While HR may want to blame the veteran—and the individual service member does need to get smarter about developing their civilian resumes—we as managers and HR professionals need to get better at interpreting these military resumes. If we don't make the effort, we can't claim the prize of bringing on board a phenomenal new employee.

Currently there are three basic resume formats in use: chronological, functional, and a hybrid of the two. Each has its pluses and minuses, and at the end of the day recruiters have their own preferences for one format or another. That being said, studies show the chronological format to be most commonly used and preferred by recruiters.

The chronological format presents a professional development trajectory over time, in which the earliest job is often the most junior, followed by roles of increasing skill and responsibility. The reader can infer, therefore, that the first job listed—the most recent job—represents the highest level of mastery and accomplishment in a candidate's career.

However (and here's the rub), a military career doesn't necessarily progress this way. For example, responsibility for a large staff may be viewed by civilian employers as a sign of strong leadership experience. But for a career service member, that large staff may have been three jobs ago . . . and followed by roles that were smaller in scope from a staff management perspective but much greater in scope of access to people and information, influencing leaders and strategy, etc. So a civilian recruiter could potentially read this evolution in the chronological resume as a backward step in leadership ability.

This explains why so many former military personnel become frustrated in their early civilian roles. The recruiting process focuses on the most recent job on the resume, which prevents the organization from recognizing, hiring, and leveraging the full contribution of the service member. The conceptual shift we are called to make is to look at a military resume through a different lens, even if—perhaps especially if—both are in chronological format. This is how we can see the full value of a military career and compare it to other candidates coming from civilian or academic careers.

> "If you're only using the new-hire for what he did in his last job, you're going to miss out on a lot of capabilities and experiences that that individual has that could help the firm. Even in areas that are unanticipated. For example, I'm doing a job right now that was completely unanticipated. The second thing is for the individual. He or she is going to be frustrated by the fact that he or she has skills that aren't being used and mostly because the organization doesn't know he or she has those skills or experiences."
>
> —OFFICER, USAF[1]

Think of it this way: a civilian career often looks like a climb up from one position to another, better position; the military career can look like a trek through various positions whose importance does not necessarily proceed vertically but, rather, laterally across time.

FIGURE 10.2

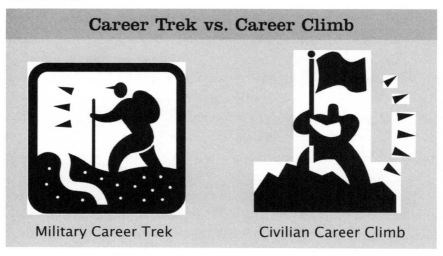

Military Career Trek   Civilian Career Climb

Do you need to become fully fluent in "militarese" to hire veterans? No. Do you need to work differently to understand what veterans bring to the table? Definitely. If you don't completely understand what you're reading on a resume, how do you figure it out? The quickest, easiest way is to enlist the help of veterans who already work in your organization. Individuals will likely be happy to help you translate the resume of a fellow service member. If your organization has an employee resource group (ERG) for veterans, they can make a tangible contribution by providing support with resume translation, candidate interviewing, and new-hire mentoring programs.

In lieu of existing employees with military experience, here are a few primary resources on the subject of translating a military resume:

- To identify military jobs that map to the civilian positions you are trying to fill, go to O*Net Online: www.onetonline.org. This is an online service available through the U.S. Department of Labor and is a great place to start.

- To understand the military rank structure, awards, and other designations, I have used *A Civilian's Guide to the U.S. Military,* by Barbara Schading

- To translate terms and acronyms you may see on military resumes, check out *Military-to-Civilian Resumes and Letters,* by Carl Savino and Ronald Krannich.

Interviewing Candidates

The interview is how you're going to get the information you need about the military job candidate. Because you don't read "militarese" and the candidate neither translates into civilian nor has experience interviewing for jobs, your ability to ask the right questions will be key to success, for both you and the veteran. It is well worth any extra time and effort you may need to put into the interview if you get the best possible candidate for the job you're filling.

Here are a few basics to consider, courtesy of a few veterans:

"Take the time to explain to potential candidates about the hiring process. Most of the time this is the military person's first encounter with a corporate recruiter and I think a lot of military personnel get nervous dealing with the recruiter because they don't know or understand the hiring process."

—ENLISTED SERVICE MEMBER, USMC[2]

"If you know you're hiring a former military person . . . realize they had a lot of responsibility, worked under stress and pressure, and can probably offer a lot more leadership capacity than others. You have to help harness it."

—ENLISTED SERVICE MEMBER, USAF[3]

"Explain that many positions that they will consider won't be for management and they may have to start at the technical level while they hone and demonstrate their managerial skills."

—ENLISTED SERVICE MEMBER, US ARMY[4]

Below are seven secrets to success when interviewing military job candidates:

1. *Do your homework.* During the interview you will be asking the candidate to translate his or her military experience into civilian terms, so it is only fair that you, the hiring or HR manager, be prepared to explain the job opening in jargon-free terms. Also, come prepared to describe:

   a. What success looks like in the job.
   b. What success looks like in the organization.
   c. The personality of the organization as a whole (otherwise known as culture).

Use what you've learned in this book to anticipate questions the candidate may have and to offer insight and information that the candidate may not know to ask for. Finally, educate yourself as to the basics of the military rank structure so you know who to look for when you screen resumes and candidates. For example, if you want to fill an entry-level position, a candidate who left service as a non-commissioned officer (e.g., E-8) might not be the best long-term fit. This is not to discourage you from considering every promising candidate, simply to increase your odds of retention by making relative comparisons between the civilian role and previous military rank.

2. *Suspend judgments about the candidate based on his or her resume.* See previous reference to career trek vs. career climb!

3. *Focus on capability rather than equivalent job history.* Ask about the types of tools and technology used, the types of equipment licenses and training received. When looking at the job requisition you're trying to fill, think in terms of essential job functions rather than "nice to have" degrees and certifications.

> "It is too easy for a prospective employer to say 'He drove a tank. We don't have tanks here.' This same employer does not understand that the tank has a computer, laser, radar, whatever. It is not

a tank but a highly complicated piece of equipment. Similar to a piece of lab equipment or a production line component. Line Management needs to have the ability to look ahead when interviewing a veteran: 'This vet served his country for X-number of years. He has proven he is teachable and trainable. Our company needs employees that we can train and teach who will stay with us.' This is some of the value veterans bring to civilian employers."

—ENLISTED SERVICE MEMBER, US NAVY[5]

"Ask about the decisions and choices the veteran had to make . . . look beyond education. Many veterans have more worldly experience than they are given credit for. Figure out how to weigh and give credit for military experience and utilize the talent that's there."

—ENLISTED SERVICE MEMBER, USAF[6]

"Ask what they did, how the experiences helped them, and how they could help a company. E-4+ have some type of supervisory experience whether they realize it or not. Ask what they did to help those they supervised."

—ENLISTED SERVICE MEMBER, US NAVY[7]

Further, push hiring managers to think in these terms as well, lest they pass over outstanding candidates. (The other side of this coin is that some veterans will pass you by as potential employers if they see a list of requirements they can't meet. It won't be obvious to them which are essential vs. desired.)

See the sample Interview Questions in Figure 10.3 on page 120 to help you glean the best information from every candidate.

4. *Ask for the story.* The previous section on resumes gives us a big clue about how to interview: we need to view the candidate's military career as a whole rather than culminating in the most recent position he or she held. Armed with this insight, we simply need to draw the

story out of the candidate, stopping as often as needed to clarify what's not clear. Think of it as a process of mutual discovery. Ask about key skills learned and used in the different jobs, about the results that were achieved and the impact of those results on the mission. And, to get a bird's-eye view of the individual's commitment, determination, and grit, ask about the barriers he or she had to overcome in order to get the job done.

5. *Describe the job.* You and the candidate have mutually supportive goals: you need to fill a position and he or she needs a job. A spirit of collaboration can be helpful in the interview process, as a way of putting you both at ease and making the most of the interview time. I suggest placing the job description beside the candidate's resume so you can reference back and forth and figure it out together. Remember that you are recruiting for retention here, so don't oversell the position or the organization just to close the requisition. Our surveys of former service members tell us that they tend to become disillusioned if the job is not how it was described during the interview process, and they will quit due to lack of fit with the organizational culture. The same could probably be said of all job candidates, but it really holds true with service members. We must establish realistic expectations of the place and the role in order to recruit for retention.

6. *Use behavioral interview questions.* Describe a scenario and ask the candidate how he or she would respond to it. Or ask the candidate to describe a scenario and how he or she accomplished the objective or overcame an obstacle. This lets you in on how the individual assesses and responds to situations that could arise in the course of doing the job you're trying to fill. The key here is to limit the scenarios to things that could or would occur—keep them relevant. Not sure where to start? You can always open with a word of thanks for the candidate's military service.

7. *Ask about community-building activities.* Military job candidates may not think to mention them but you should because they speak volumes. Because military life includes work, family, and community,

many things we civilians might call team-building or employee-appreciation events are standard weekend activity for service members. Planning and coordinating a cookout for five hundred or cleanup of a ten-mile stretch of shoreline is no big deal. Further, many military roles and missions involve community building at local levels. Therefore, you will learn a lot about the candidate's abilities by asking about this type of activity. It will fill out the picture of true leadership experience by illustrating how the candidate took something from concept to execution, built coalitions of support, leveraged resources, conquered interpersonal barriers, and led a team to success.

If you hire or plan to hire former military officers, keep in mind that there are three types of military officers: commissioned or general officers (entered the military as officers, following college, usually a military academy), non-commissioned officers or NCOs (entered the military at the very lowest enlisted rank and progressed to the highest enlisted rank, supporting commissioned officers), and warrant officers (senior enlisted specialists). The span of control and responsibility is different for each type, so be sure to inquire during the interview process as to actual duties performed.

Making the Hire

This is an important time to remember that the person you are going to hire does not have a lot of experience evaluating job offers. In the military, you go where they send you and where you're needed, and you learn to do the job at hand. In exchange for this service, the military handles all your benefits, taxes, salary adjustments, etc. Be careful not to make assumptions about the candidate's understanding of logistical details, and take extra care to ask questions and answer questions. Often, the military new-hire lived and worked on a base that also held a gymnasium, dining, shopping, and other facilities in one common area. Be sure to cover the basics, even if they seem obvious to you. See page 121 for things to cover in addition to benefits.

FIGURE 10.3

Interview Questions

Your goal is to understand the various roles, responsibilities, skills, and experience the candidate has accumulated over the course of his or her military career. To do this, you may need to look well beyond the most recent position, going back ten years. Remember, unlike a civilian resume that often culminates in the highest level of responsibility to date, the military resume must be viewed as a collection of experiences to be considered together as a whole.

1. General opening questions, to build rapport and sense where the individual is in his or her transition from military service to civilian employment: "I know leaving the military can be a big transition . . ."
   - How is it going, separating from military service?
   - How has the adjustment been?
   - What has been the biggest surprise about the civilian workplace?
   - What opportunities are you looking forward to taking advantage of as a civilian employee?
   - What challenges do you foresee as a new civilian employee?

2. For each job over the past ten years, ask:
   - How would you describe this position in layman's terms?
   - What was your primary mission in this job?
   - What did it take to accomplish this mission?
   - What were the key activities you performed, and in what circumstances?
   - What people or resources were you responsible for in this role?
   - What were the greatest challenges in the role?
   - What is an example of a time that everything went as planned?
     - What was your contribution?
     - What did you learn from the experience?
     - How did you incorporate what worked and what you learned?

- What is an example of a time that things did not go as planned?
  - What went wrong?
  - What did you do? (What was your contribution?)
  - What did you learn from the experience?
  - What did you change or do differently as a result of this experience?
- What aspects of this role or job would you like to find in a civilian position?
- What aspects of this role or job would you prefer not to perform in a civilian position?

3. General questions:
   - How would you approach a situation in which _____ (describe something "typical" of the job the interview is applying for)?
   - What kinds of things did you coordinate and accomplish in the community (e.g., community social events, charitable projects, leadership roles)?
   - Looking across your recent (past ten years) military work experiences, what key knowledge, skills, abilities, and experiences would you say are most valuable?
     - Setting aside the specific job you were required to do, what activities do these knowledge, skills, abilities, and experiences prepare you to do?
     - How do you imagine yourself applying them in a civilian setting?

Areas to be covered in addition to benefits:

- Where they should report for work on their first day, and at what time
- Manager's name and contact information
- Forms they need to turn in, when, and to whom
- What if anything they need to bring

- Dress code
- What they should expect in the first days and weeks of learning and trying to perform

On a related note, this will likely be the first time the service member has been in a position to negotiate for a higher salary, which many civilian recruiters bank on as a way of keeping costs low. However, this can trigger the hire-replace cycle when the new employee learns that his or her colleagues earn more for the same job. It may be distasteful to think of employees as talking about such things, but in the military it is transparent; salary is literally an open book. If the recruiter is misleading or takes advantage of the service member's lack of civilian experience, it can easily reflect badly on the whole organization and draw a bold black line between you and attrition. The military is large but the community of veterans is close. To avoid becoming known as a bad place to work, and to ensure you become known as a veteran-friendly employer of choice, you have to do the right thing during the hiring process by making a fair and competitive offer.

Recruitment and the Wounded Warrior

Wounded Warrior is a term currently used to describe someone returning from combat with some type of injury, visible or otherwise. By visible I mean injuries obvious to the observer, such as loss of limb, paralysis, or burns. By "otherwise" I refer to TBI and PTSD, discussed in Part 1 of the book. The Veterans Administration has a complex model for determining degree of disability but, for our purposes here, let's assume that anyone with a combat injury is a Wounded Warrior.

When it comes to recruitment, there are a few key things you want to consider about Wounded Warriors: how to find them, how to interview them, and how to accommodate them. Most of what you know about the Americans with Disability Act (ADA) applies to this population, so be sure to refresh your understanding of it.

In terms of how to find Wounded Warrior candidates, there is the passive approach and the active approach. The passive approach refers to the occasions in which they seek you out as a potential employer. For example, by submitting an online resume or attending a job fair. In this case, you may or may not know the candidate's injured status, especially if his or her injury is not visibly obvious. Candidates may not choose to disclose it, as is their prerogative, and you can't ask. The importance of this point is that you may be interviewing and hiring Wounded Warriors without even realizing it. This is no different than any job candidate (with or without a military background) whose disability is not evident and who chooses not to disclose it.

The active approach to recruiting and hiring Wounded Warriors is to seek them out through sourcing channels designed to facilitate their entry to the workplace. Examples include the Wounded Warrior Project and the U.S. Department of Labor. When you source a candidate through such a pipeline, in which their injured status is made transparent to potential employers, the Wounded Warrior may initiate discussion of his or her injury. As an employer, you may ask what if any reasonable accommodation is needed to complete the recruiting process, but that's where your questioning about the disability or injury ends.

In many cases, Wounded Warrior candidates are young, with less than 10 years of military service. Their combat injury will likely bring a premature end to what they'd hoped would be a long career of military service. As such, they may be less prepared to enter the civilian workplace, and be less confident than their civilian peers in terms of their own marketability and contribution. Therefore, Wounded Warrior candidates may appear less polished and confident in the interview process. Likely, they are juggling treatment and rehabilitation along with their job search, not to mention separating from military service, so there is a lot in play for them when they initially sit down to discuss employment opportunities.

Tips for recruiting Wounded Warriors include:

- Make the effort to find them, as they will not likely find you on their own
- Think about open positions in terms of essential job functions and core capabilities rather than looking only for equivalent experience
- Ensure jobs for Wounded Warriors can be structured flexibly, as often the only accommodation an individual will need is the flexibility to attend to medical appointments during the work day or to work a modified schedule
- Ensure hiring managers are supportive of the flexibility described above, and prepared to accommodate (if not, the job itself may not be a good fit)
- Be prepared to talk about the physical work environment (e.g., working in a private office versus working in a loud bullpen setting makes a difference in terms of managing distraction and interruption)
- Ensure anyone who will be conducting interviews (e.g., recruiters, line managers) are informed on ADA regulations beforehand
- Educate interviewers and hiring managers on the facts about Wounded Warriors (e.g., not everyone has PTSD, reasonable accommodations are generally not cost prohibitive) and address any resistance they may have based on misinformation

Closing Thoughts

Former military service members are a tremendous untapped pool of talent in the job market. They bring qualities and values that can't

text continues on page 127

FIGURE 10.4

Putting It All Together
Conversations on Both Sides of the Fence

Service members chatting at the commissary . . .

Army buddy to job candidate: "Hey, how did the big interview go today?"

Possible response 1: "Not so great. It was over really quickly and I didn't really understand what she was looking for. She asked a bunch of questions about my last tour of duty, available start date, and details like that. She didn't say too much about the open position."

Possible response 2: "Great! It was quick and painless, the interviewer got right down to business and even asked when I'd be available to start! That's got to be a good sign, right?"

A week later . . .

Army buddy: "So, did you get the job?"

Probable response: "I don't know, I haven't heard anything. I left a follow up voice message and email, but they didn't even give me the courtesy of a reply!"

Recruiters chatting at company headquarters . . .

Recruiting manager to recruiter: "How did the job fair go today at the base?"

Possible response 1: "Total waste of time. If I have to look at another five-page resume full of alphabet soup, I will lose it. The candidates didn't have many transferable skills. They obviously researched the company, which was good, but didn't have a lot of questions."

Possible response 2: "I'm not sure . . . most of the candidates seemed kind of shy, and you had to pull the information out of them. Everyone was nice enough, but I don't know if they can do our jobs."

A week later . . .

Recruiting manager: "So, where are we with the candidates from the base?"

Probable response: "Ugh, they keep calling me to follow up, as if they are the only candidates and these are the only jobs we are trying to fill!"

FIGURE 10.5

Putting It All Together
Assess the Conversations

What do you think was the biggest mistake
on the part of the . . .

Candidate	*Recruiter*

What few things could have made a positive difference
on the part of the . . .

Candidate	*Recruiter*

really be taught. Your organization may really benefit from hiring veterans, and veterans may really benefit from being part of your organization. But you have to overcome the communication and cultural divide in order to get on the same page. Veteran-friendly employers of choice understand this and know it is worth the effort.

You need to have an authentic story about your organization that is attractive to former service members. The more authentic that story is, and the more you recruit with retention in mind, the more likely you are to make a great hire. And that is a win-win: The employee will have a long and rewarding career and your organization will recruit and retain an employee who adds value and provides a return on the recruiting investment. Oh, and to tell his or her military buddies what a great place yours is to work!

FIGURE 10.6

Closing Activity

List three ideas you came up with to improve the HR/
recruitment processes in your organization, relative to
hiring veterans:

1. _____
_____
_____
_____
_____
_____

2. _____
_____
_____
_____
_____
_____

3. _____
_____
_____
_____
_____
_____

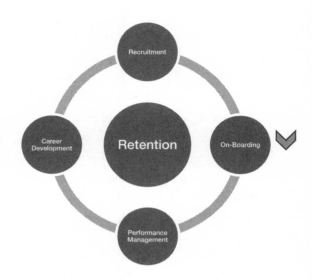

CHAPTER 11

On-Boarding

ON-BOARDING IS THE PROCESS of bringing a new-hire up to speed as an employee of your organization. There is no one right way to do this. Large organizations tend to have formal structures for on-boarding, such as an orientation training class, while small organizations tend to be less formal and may limit on-boarding to walking the new hire around to meet everyone in the office. The expectation is that all that needs to be learned will be learned on the job, rather than in a classroom. This chapter focuses on:

- The connection between on-boarding and retention
- On-boarding needs of veterans
- Eight great tips for on-boarding veterans
- An opportunity to apply what you've read to four real-life scenarios.

The Connection Between On-Boarding and Retention

On-boarding is important because it contributes to retention. It is, after all, the new employee's first impression of the organization with which he or she has found employment. *The interest and effort put into receiving the new-hire is an organization's greatest opportunity to build a bond and engage the employee as a loyal member of the team, rather than just another interchangeable worker.* Employee engagement is an ongoing need to retain your talent, and it cannot be accomplished in a day. Rather, it should be embedded into the objectives of all employee programs and messaging. An employee who feels part of an organization she admires is more likely to stay than one who feels disconnected or undervalued. This is especially true for former service members who experienced "extreme" on-boarding in the military in the form of boot camp or officer candidate school!

> "There needs to be some guidance on how to work in the civilian world, especially for people who went into the military after high school and it's all they know . . . they think that's how the world operates."
>
> —ENLISTED SERVICE MEMBER, USAF[1]

Smart companies are reframing on-boarding as a series of activities and events that occur throughout an individual's first twelve months of employment. Busy people learn best when the lessons coincide with their need for information. Therefore, inundating a room full of new-hires with an introduction to the company from A to Z will not yield optimal results, as the new-hires can only take in so much. Providing information and training when it can be applied is a better approach than overwhelming new-hires with anything and everything there is to know about your organization.

Be deliberate about planning your on-boarding strategy. If you decide not to offer a class, have a rationale for the decision and offer another way to get people up to speed quickly. If you decide to offer a more formal program like a class, ensure it is relevant and applicable rather than a "check-the-box" activity. Investing a bit of time in a discussion of what new employees need and want in order to be successful quickly pays dividends in the form of retention.

On-Boarding Needs of Veterans

Nowhere is on-boarding more important than with former military service members. They need organizational context in addition to information specific to mission and vision. Remember, veterans are coming from a very strong culture in which most processes and procedures are codified and explicit. Is this how you would describe your organization? If not, chances are good you will need to spend some time making the implicit explicit, explaining things that seem obvious to you or that are obvious to new-hires coming from nonmilitary organizations. While every organization's culture and operations are different, those differences are small compared to the quantum difference between military culture and civilian culture.

> "I think if either an individual coach or a formal class was provided to these people coming out of the military saying, 'Hey, this is what our organization is all about, here's how we operate, here's how we are different from the military and things you need to be aware of' early in their tenure, it would be very helpful. It would have been huge for me; I wouldn't have floundered so much my first year or been so frustrated or tempted to leave my company."
>
> —OFFICER, USAF[2]

> "[Veterans] are leaving an extremely regimented world for a [civilian] world where they have a voice, and commanding everyone is not necessary or accepted. There will be a definite need for molding and counseling during this adjustment but their dedication, diligence, and determination to achieving the goal is worth it."
>
> —ENLISTED SERVICE MEMBER, US ARMY[3]

> "I think many lower enlisted personnel don't understand finances as well as they should for the civilian world. Many things in the military such as healthcare, etc., are taken care of for them. I think they should understand taxable income and how much comes

from their paychecks to cover many of the benefits that were previously given to them."

—ENLISTED SERVICE MEMBER, US NAVY[4]

Your on-boarding approach for veterans doesn't have to be elabo-
rate. As I said earlier, the most important thing is that you give it some
thought and advanced preparation. It should scale to your business
needs and objectives. *If you only hire one or two veterans a year, then think
about having a one-to-one chat once a week for the first month as well as
providing the new-hires with resources to peruse on their own.* If you hire lots
of service members or know that you are going to in the near future
(e.g., because of a new client contract or organizational initiative),
think about something more formally structured, like an orientation/
transition class during the first day or week of employment.

Whatever the right size and structure for you may be, it is key to
have the veteran in mind and feature information he or she is not
likely to know or even think about (e.g., that your organization has a
formal structure but is flexible with the market and can shift every
eighteen months or so). A few examples of how to implement tailored
on-boarding are:

- Develop a stand-alone on-boarding program for veterans.
- Integrate content for veterans with existing new-hire orientation
  material.
- Compile an information packet for new-hires who are veterans, to
  include:
  - info about the organization's purpose, structure, and clients
    served
  - info about the new-hire's division or team, what it does, and
    how that supports the larger organization's goals
  - info about the new-hire's role on the team and clients to be
    served
  - how employee performance is measured
  - vocabulary/language

Eight Great Tips for On-Boarding Veterans

1. *Assign a learning buddy.* Before the employee's first day on the job, assign someone to show him or her the ropes for the first few weeks. Remember, a lot of what you assume service members will know from previous experience will be wrong, so position them for success early by anticipating needs.

2. *Assign a mentor.* Who better to make the translation between military and civilian ways of operating than another veteran who has gone before and made a successful transition? The military are a helpful bunch, especially when it comes to helping their own; your current employees who previously served will likely jump at the chance to mentor a "newbie." This will not only accelerate learning but strengthen the bond between the new-hire and your organization because it is a show of support. Military organizations typically assign a mentor to junior personnel, so this is a comfortable role for veterans to take on. Ensure the roles of mentor and mentee are clear, with accountabilities in place to guarantee purposeful interaction and outcomes.

3. *Engage the family.* One thing that differentiates the military from the civilian way of life is the involvement of family. Because military service is a twenty-four/seven operation and one likely lives on the base where one works, the boundaries between work life and personal life overlap. The result is a strong sense of community that includes the whole family. So to help with the transition and engaging new-hires early, including a veteran's spouse makes a real difference. If you're a manager taking the new-hire to lunch on his first day, why not invite his partner to join as well? If orientation activities or materials can include the partner it will go a long way toward early engagement of the employee.

4. *Set expectations.* The previous chapter on recruitment talked about the importance of setting clear expectations during the interview process to avoid unpleasant surprises down the line. The same

goes for the on-boarding process. It is another key opportunity to clarify expectations and organizational norms and to prepare the service member for early success. *Remember, veterans come to you from a different world, culturally speaking, so check your assumptions at the door in terms of what they'll know about your organization's world, and make the implicit explicit.* Consider the suggestion of an enlisted USMC:[5]

"Many enlisted are used to being told when they could leave work. This isn't the case as a civilian. The civilian manager should explain the basic rules for arriving at work, when they can leave, lunch breaks, dress code, cultural norms, etc."

As for another example, you might say something like, "I value your skill and experience in this line of work, and want to ensure your success by letting you know how we think about and do the work here at Company X."

5. *Give a warm welcome.* I wish I had a dollar for every time I've heard about a new employee showing up on his or her first day, only to be met with a blank stare as if no one knew they had been hired. The few minutes it takes to scurry around and find out who this new person is and where she's supposed to go makes a lasting first impression . . . and not the good kind. This goes for any new employee, of course, but especially for the service member who may already feel like a bit of an outsider on day one. If you accept the premise that on-boarding is key to retention because it builds an early bond, then you'll understand how small oversights can have big impacts. Start things off on the right foot by anticipating the veteran's first day of employment and being prepared to receive him or her.

6. *Check in periodically.* Because service members "don't know what they don't know" about civilian operations and culture, it often won't occur to them to ask about how to do their jobs. Rather, like most new-hires, veterans learn a lot by making mistakes and potentially embarrassing faux pas. And because service members come to their civilian organizations with years of work experience, it is easy for us to assume they know how to operate effectively and that they'll ask if

they don't. The issue is not usually job knowledge but understanding *how* a job gets done in your environment. Chances are the nuts and bolts of accomplishing work are different from how work is accomplished in the military, so it is crucial that you as the manager or internal HR professional check in with the new employee periodically to gauge how things are going, answer questions, address concerns, check assumptions, and calibrate expectations. Additionally, use these touch points to establish a strong personal connection and build engagement.

7. *Utilize the Manager's Mid-Year Check-In™*. Line managers and HR professionals have a great new tool at their disposal with this quick and easy assessment.* Intended to be filled out by the service member's manager at or around the six-month mark, the Mid-Year Check-In™ is a management tool to gauge performance and fit before the first formal review (most companies perform some type of annual performance assessment). This ensures that feedback is being given and properly implemented and opens the door to conversation about how the employee's transition is progressing and what, if any, challenges or opportunities for which he or she may need guidance. Early pulse checks can help you avoid situations like this one, so common among new-hires and especially former military:

"I was assigned work to do and left to go do it. Now, after knowing more about my actual tasks, this was fine, but for a long time I wasn't confident that I was moving ahead in the same direction as management on my tasks and dealings with other company employees." Enlisted, USN[6]

The early pulse check is also a good time to check in regarding emerging needs for reasonable accommodation, or effectiveness of existing accommodations.

8. *Connect them to a community*. A growing trend in large civilian organizations is to sponsor a forum of some sort (sometimes called an

---

*available at www.militarytransitions.biz

affiliation or networking group) for employees who served in the military. It provides veterans with the sense of community they may miss, encourages networking and collaboration, and, again, builds a bond to the organization. Sometimes things we're uncomfortable asking about are more easily addressed with someone who has shared our life experience. This is not unique to veterans; smart companies find that providing such forums serve other groups as well, such as women and minority groups. It doesn't have to cost much; in fact, all it takes is one person willing to organize an occasional get-together. Some organizations are using Skype as an affordable way of connecting their veterans; others sponsor employee affiliation groups to facilitate networking and develop community among veterans. Take care, however, not to overuse such groups to the degree that they become a point of division rather than a point of diversity and inclusion.

On-Boarding and Wounded Warriors

When it comes to on-boarding Wounded Warriors, there are three or four primary factors I recommend considering. Beyond these, everything I've already said about on-boarding veterans (and any new-hire, for that matter), applies.

First, it is very important to spell out the resources available through your organization, specifically, Employee Assistance Programs (EAP), corporate health and wellness services, health benefits, and resources in place to support employees with disabilities. These will all be new concepts to former military personnel, and can make a real difference in augmenting any services they may be receiving from the Veterans Administration.

Second, and related to the first suggestion, is inviting the Wounded Warrior to include a parent or spouse in these discussions as a demonstration of support for your new employee. Civilian programs and resources can be a bit of a mystery the first time around, and it can be a comfort to have a second pair of ears listening in to ensure all is understood.

Third, if you have an Employee Resource Group (ERG) for veterans, engage its members early in the on-boarding process. Connecting the Wounded Warrior to a community within the civilian organization has been linked to retention. If you do not have an ERG in place, consider reaching out to other veterans who work for your organization to enroll them in the on-boarding process for fellow veterans.

Fourth, in addition to or instead of engaging a veterans' ERG, line up a learning buddy for your Wounded Warrior new-hire (as you might for any new-hire), to be a source of support, information, and insight in the earliest days and weeks of employment.

Closing Thoughts

You may have noticed that many of the "great eight" tips listed above have relevance and value to most new employees, not just former service members. But they are likely to have greater impact on the veteran. Even those service members who have had a previous civilian job may well benefit. This is why smart companies are engaging their Diversity and Inclusion teams in on-boarding veterans; they realize that one size does not fit all.

Now, if you really want to hit it out of the park and stand out as a veteran-friendly employer of choice, you'll put some thought into preparing your organization to integrate service members by providing information and awareness along the way (versus just when hired). Many employees will not have worked with or personally have known a veteran before and may be surprised by the cultural norms they bring with them from the military. During the transition process—that is, as your organization transitions into a veteran-friendly organization—it can be useful to think about messaging and resources for nonveteran employees regarding working with veterans. Consider providing employees with some basic information about veterans. For example, you can put together a "Military Basics" training module or, for an even more economical solution, distribute the special-edition *InfoLine* booklet titled "On-Boarding Veterans into the Civilian Workplace," published by the American Society for Training and Development (ASTD).

FIGURE 11.1

Putting It All Together
On-Boarding Scenarios

Read each of the following scenarios—based on real clients—
and respond to the question that follows. The objective is to
avoid misunderstanding and assumptions by explaining things
clearly and making the implicit in your organization explicit.

Scenario 1
A senior manager is passed up for promotion after six years
of loyal service to a civilian employer. Based on a prior military
career, his expectation has always been that good deeds would
be recognized and rewarded. In fact, while his employer appre-
ciates him, the veteran has never articulated his career goals
and aspirations. It hadn't dawned on him to toot his own horn
to progress in the company. In the veteran's words, "I didn't
know how to advocate for myself because I'd never had to do
it in the military."

**Question: How would you describe your organization's
promotion philosophy?**

_____
_____
_____
_____
_____
_____
_____

Tip: Use the Manager's Mid-Year Check-In™.

Scenario 2
A corporate trainer with a wealth of functional expertise from
her military career does a great job on every task she is given.
However, when not specifically assigned a task, she is non-
productive and awaits further instruction. Her first civilian performance evaluation calls out a lack of initiative. In this case,

the employer's expectation that staff be self-directed was counterintuitive for the veteran. After all, her military career—and very survival—required that all actions be planned and executed to the letter. Initiative in this context would have been met with a harsh reprimand. In her own words, "I didn't get it: I had done everything I'd been told to do and did it well. In between tasks I read the paper or surfed the Web. Little did I know this was viewed as slacking off!"

Question: How would you describe your organization's expectations related to initiative?

_____

_____

_____

_____

_____

_____

_____

Tip: Make the implicit explicit.

Scenario 3
A young man with seven years of service as an enlisted infantryman quits his first three civilian jobs after spending less than three years in each. A recruiter asks why he quits every job after so little time, warning that future employers would see it as a red flag. The recruiter asks why he didn't seek other internal roles rather than leaving the organizations altogether. In his own words, "In the military you change jobs every three years, so it was getting to be that time. I don't think my civilian managers even knew who I was, so it didn't occur to me to ask them if I was allowed to look for other jobs internally."

Question: When and how would you discuss such career options with a new-hire?

_____

_____

_____

_____

continues

_____

_____

_____

Tip: Find a balance between giving information as it is needed and giving information in advance so new-hires have it to review at their leisure.

Scenario 4
A retired officer, now a successful civilian executive, develops a reputation in the civilian world as a taskmaster with a "my way or the highway" attitude, not listening to the perspectives of those junior to him. Top-performing, high-potential team members are rumored to be actively job hunting. At the manager's one-year mark, he is instructed to modify his behavior to be less dictatorial, and he is given an executive coach. In his own words, "In the military mission always comes first. You definitely try to take care of your people but it is always 'Get the mission done regardless of the impact to the people.'"

Question: How does this work in your organization?

_____

_____

_____

_____

_____

_____

Tip: Use the examples in chapter 7 to explain the role of mission and relationship.

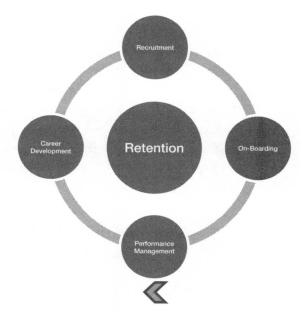

CHAPTER 12

Performance Management

THERE ARE A WEALTH OF BOOKS on managing employee performance and I won't reinvent the wheel here, but rather I will focus on the aspects that are unique to veterans. As with the other topics covered in this book, you can apply much of the thinking to other employee groups as well, so that you increase overall retention. However, I'll explain how and why the concepts are especially important for your veterans. Specifically, this chapter looks at:

- The link between performance management and retention
- Explaining metrics
- Success factors and derailers
- Manager's Mid-Year Check-In™
- Feedback mechanisms and approach
- Managing and leading staff

Performance Management and Retention

As you already know by now, military service members are used to executing against a mission. There is a sense of importance and an expectation of excellence (remember the stakes). Therefore, veterans will want and expect to be as successful as a civilian employee of your organization. To the extent you can accelerate the cultural learning curve for veterans and support their on-the-job success, you will positively impact retention. If, on the other hand, the veteran is left to sink or swim, to learn every lesson the hard way—through real-time trial and error—and to feel alone in the drive for success, the organization can hold itself accountable for premature attrition.

Don't get me wrong. Service members are quick learners and accustomed to using their wits and experience to figure things out on the fly. This approach works in the military because:

- Everyone is working together toward shared goals.
- Everyone has a common understanding of roles and performance standards.
- A team of peers and leaders is fully vested in the success of the individual.

How similar is this to your organization's culture? Chances are, you are hitting the mark to some extent on one or more of the elements. But because your organization's mission is different from the military's mission, it probably looks a bit different. That's fine; the goal is not to change your organization's culture to sync with what the veteran is used to. The goal is to set and manage the veteran's expectations at the front end, clarifying how and why success occurs differently than in the military. Here are some tips from the front:

> "Most veterans are self-motivated because they have a sense of duty and professionalism to perform and get the job done. Don't micro-manage them. Many, especially if they ranked E-6 or above, have had experience leading and directing others. Give them the task, the authority to accomplish it, any parameters they need to work within, and let them do what they do best."
>
> —ENLISTED SERVICE MEMBER, USAF[1]

"Challenge them. Service members are used to goals and objectives. Give them some along with certain parameters and then let them go. Reel them back in as necessary, but chances are they will deliver results you did not expect."

—ENLISTED SERVICE MEMBER, US COAST GUARD[2]

Explaining Metrics

While many service members have experience managing budgets, staff, and resources, they do not have experience doing it in a context that measures performance daily on the New York Stock Exchange. For this reason, priorities are different regarding metrics, and you want to be clear about what they are in your organization.

Remember the translator tool from chapter two (select a *word or concept* used by your organization, interpret the word or concept according to its *practical meaning*, further break down the word or concept into *concrete behaviors* that exemplify it, and articulate the organization's formal or stated expectations)? It can be very helpful in breaking down how performance is measured in your organization. Useful for all new employees: yes. Essential for former service members: absolutely. Performance metrics are thought of differently in the military, with greater emphasis placed on impact to the mission and meeting grade-level expectations versus entrepreneurialism, business development, and risk taking.

I recommend a one-to-one sit-down or group training for military new-hires that clearly explains, step by step, your organization's philosophy and practice regarding:

- Defining performance (e.g., five core competencies)
- Measuring performance (e.g., five-point rating scale; 360-degree input)
- Measuring impact (e.g., what results does activity yield for the organization?)

- Assessing performance (e.g., six-month check-in in the first year, followed by an annual review)
- Assigning meaning (e.g., a rating of "on track" is considered acceptable in year one, but the employee must meet the minimum standard in year two)
- Rewarding performance (e.g., a rating of "on track" in year one equates to a 3 percent raise)
- Developing capability (e.g., available training, action planning)
- Correcting performance gaps (e.g., six-month window to resolve issues)

Hopefully you are having this conversation with all new-hires. Regardless, you or someone on your team needs to articulate performance expectations to new-hires from the military. Their only frame of reference is what's generally referred to as a "military fitness report," which aims to track the effectiveness of a massive number of personnel in the most efficient manner possible. The military culture values giving corrective feedback verbally rather than in writing, and in real time. This is important to know for two reasons:

1. If your organization provides corrective or "developmental" feedback in writing, it will come as an unpleasant shock to the veteran and create needless anxiety.
2. If your organization's culture does not value or do a good job of providing real-time feedback, but rather saves it up for the annual review, the veteran will likely feel blindsided (as anyone might).

It isn't hard to see how one or both of these experiences could undermine a veteran's feeling of being supported and positioned to succeed. New employees expect a learning curve but need to feel successful within a reasonable period of time if they are to remain motivated. Clearly establishing the veteran's expectations around measurement of and support for performance is critical to retention.

Success Factors and Derailers

In addition to formal performance metrics, your organization proba-bly has a lot of unwritten wisdom about what works and what doesn't. I'm referring to the cultural aspects of performance management, the "real" way to get things done successfully. To the extent it is possible to codify some of this wisdom for the benefit of new-hires, it's worth the time and effort spent *making the implicit explicit*. When organiza-tional clients ask me to do this for them, my preferred method is to conduct focus groups with staff at different grades who are, of course, former service members. Sample questions are:

- Regarding Performance Management, what do you wish someone here had told you in your:
  - first day?
  - first week?
  - first year?
- What words of advice would you give a service member joining the company?
- What is one thing a new-hire should absolutely do (success factor) and absolutely not do (derailer) in order to be successful in this organization?
- What are the biggest differences between this place and the mili-tary?
- What surprised you most, as a new employee?

Manager's Mid-Year Check-In ™

It is really important to check in with the veteran (at least) six months into employment to ensure he or she is on track and operating as intended. The Manager's Mid-Year Check-In™ is a straightforward, easy-to-use tool for assessing a veteran's transition progress.* It serves (at least) two important functions for a manager and his or her em-

*available at www.militarytransitions.biz

ployee who came from the military (even if there have been a few years and/or jobs in between):

1. Provides the manager with a structured way of reflecting on the employee's attitudes and behavior and of comparing initial impressions with current impressions. The reflection process is valuable in and of itself, but it serves another function as well, which is to update the manager's overall view of the employee in light of changes or improvements that may have occurred over the six months. For example, a manager might think something like, "Steve had a hard adjustment and still struggles. On the other hand, now that I think about it, the problem was how he communicated with junior staff, which has pretty much resolved itself since I gave him the feedback two months ago. I guess Steve really isn't struggling that much anymore." Positive reinforcement is essential with any new-hire, and especially veterans who are accustomed to assessing themselves against benchmarks over time. When you identify the benchmarks through positive or corrective feedback, they can incorporate them into their own performance standards going forward.

2. Provides the manager with a structure and language for giving feedback and talking about the organization and/or team culture. For example, a manager might say something like, "Steve, I know we've talked about your transition and I've given you feedback on a few things over the last six months. I realized while completing this check-in form that you really have made strides in your direction of junior staff since we spoke about it a couple of months ago. Nice job integrating the feedback." Or, in another scenario, the manager might say something like, "Steve, I know you've struggled with the transition and I haven't been able to put my finger on what the issue is until seeing it here in this check-in form. It has to do with being open to new ways of doing things. I still sense some resistance to our lack of formal process, and want to work with you to get more comfortable with it between now and your first annual review."

Feedback Mechanisms and Approach

You've probably seen movies in which a brusque man in uniform orders his troops to "drop and give me twenty (pushups)!" for what seems to be a minor transgression on one person's part. The response, in unison, is "Sir! Yes, Sir!" This is an example of real-time feedback in the military. As we've discussed, the culture values clear and direct communication because lives are at stake in accomplishing the organization's mission. It may take some getting used to at first, but by the time a person is done with boot camp, he or she has probably accepted this style of interaction. In the words of this enlisted Navy officer:[3]

"Feedback was faster and more clear (direct) in the military than in civilian life, leading to more stress after leaving the military. . . . Civilian managers should be told that those of us recently discharged will be fine with direct, clear feedback. We are less likely to get hurt feelings over it since constant improvement is a military theme we understand."

Your organization's manner of delivering positive and critical feedback on everyday behavior is likely a bit different from the approach used in military boot camp. Otherwise, attrition would be a lot higher! Norms for giving feedback up, down, and across (to superiors, subordinates, and peers) are probably not codified anywhere, so it is essential that military new-hires get this information through some source early on. They will, undoubtedly, need to give feedback at some time or another and may well receive it from unexpected sources (subordinates), so they need to be prepared to respond constructively.

If your new-hire has management or leadership responsibility, his or her success will be measured by how effectively he or she can influence and shape staff performance while maintaining a positive working environment. This means learning the ins and outs of how feedback is used in your organization.

"To most civilians, what they do is a job. They have another life, they have a family, they have priorities, and this is just one of the boxes of their life. Understanding that they work this in, you try to motivate them to make what they do as a job much more of a calling, or an investment that they feel committed to."

—OFFICER, US ARMY[4]

You can use the translator tool from Chapter 2 to convey this information, but I think a more effective approach is to take a few moments to complete the worksheet on the next page so you can then explain feedback methods to your military (and any) new-hires.

Coaching Performance

Coaching utilizes deep listening and thoughtful questions to help individuals find their own answers to performance challenges. Anyone can use coaching questions to help his or her peers, subordinates, or even superiors. See the list of coaching questions in Figure 12.3 on page 151. You can use those or modify them to stimulate exploration and improved performance among military new-hires.

See also the Coaching Conversation scenario at the end of this chapter.

New-Hire Managers and Leaders

Over the years I have worked with many retired general officers as they made their transition from military to civilian leadership roles. Many have told me that civilian organizations lack true leadership. Furthermore, they have complained that organizations hire them for their military leadership experience but then won't allow them to lead. Organizations, on the other hand, tell me that they invest a lot of money in retired officers and receive a very slow return on that investment because their style of leadership doesn't work in a civilian setting. So all kinds of bridges are burned and opportunities lost as the former officer assimilates into the civilian workplace.

Aligning the expectations of these respective stakeholder groups

text continues on page 152

FIGURE 12.1

Feedback Conversation

Manager: John, I'd like to talk with you about the report you submitted yesterday. I see the effort you put into it. However, it is still lacking some key components. Specifically, you've done a nice, thorough job analyzing the data and reporting the themes, but I don't see your interpretation of what it all means, what "story" the data is telling us. Do you know what I mean?

John: Yes sir, I think you are saying that you want me to include my personal opinion, right?

Manager: Yes, your educated point of view (by the way, you don't need to call me "Sir.")

John: Yes, sir. I mean, okay, I will try to stop calling you that, but habits are hard to break! [they both laugh]

John: I'm not really used to including personal opinion, since in the military the boss just needed accurate facts that he could then base his own opinion on. I don't know what I'd really have to add to that in terms of my own opinion or views.

Manager: I see what you're saying. I think we're looking for something a bit different here. One thing we value about your work in the military is familiarity with this particular topic. You bring more hands-on experience than anyone else here has, and we want to learn as much as we can from you. The team can show you how to present your opinions and views in a formal report—that's the easy part. What I want to see more of is your firsthand knowledge.

John: I think so. So, for example, the theme about process gaps . . . you want me to say why I think those gaps are occurring, based on my experience?

Manager: Yes. And take it a step further by offering suggestions and recommendations for how we can eliminate those gaps. I'd like you to demonstrate ownership of the problem with me by proposing solutions. See what I'm saying?

John: Definitely. Wow, this job is going to be even more fun than I had thought! Hope you don't regret inviting my opinions—you may need to rein me in!

Manager: Well, we'll worry about that if and when it happens. For now, I want to hear every hypothesis and suggestion you have to offer. That's why I hired you.

John: Understood. I'll get right on it and have a revised report to you by the end of today.

Manager: Great, I look forward to seeing it. Thanks.

FIGURE 12.2

Putting It All Together
Explaining Feedback

1. How do people generally give feedback in this environment?

_____

_____

_____

2. What are the most and least effective techniques for giving feedback to subordinates so they hear and act on it?

_____

_____

_____

Example: _____

_____

_____

3. What are the most and least effective techniques for giving feedback to peers so they hear and consider taking action on it?

_____

_____

_____

Example: _____

_____

_____

4. What are the most and least effective techniques for giving feedback to superiors and customers so they hear and consider taking action on it?

_____

_____

_____

Example: _____

_____

_____

FIGURE 12.3

Coaching Questions

Cultural Challenge (see also the Coaching Conversation Scenario on page 45 in chapter 3)
- How would you describe your current challenge?
- What have you tried so far to address the challenge?
- How effective was that approach?
- How is it similar to situations you faced in the military?
- How is it different?
- What have you observed others doing in response to similar challenges in this environment?
- How effective were those approaches?
- What could you do to more effectively address the current challenge?
- How would you see that playing out?
- What's the next step?

Transition Process
- Now that you've been here a week, how's it going?
- What has it been like for you, leaving military service?
- What routines from military life would you like to integrate into your civilian life?
- Is there anything I can do to help make that happen?
- What has surprised you the most about leaving military service?
- How are you coping with it?
- Would you be interested in helpful resources?

Interpersonal Challenge
- How would you describe the current situation?
- Can you give me a for-instance?
- What feedback have you received about it?
- How does the feedback about your impact align with your intended impact?
- Putting yourself in _____'s shoes, how could that have come across?
- What have you noticed about the organization [or team, or people] that can explain the gap?
- What approaches have you observed others using effectively in this environment?
- Why do you suppose that would be important?
- What would you be willing to do differently to achieve a better result?
- Is there anyone you'd feel comfortable checking in with to get some real-time feedback?

begins at the most basic level imaginable: the word "leadership." We all know the word, but are we using the same definition? No. It means completely different things in military and civilian worlds.

In the military, leadership is trained and expected from day one. It has specific boundaries and activities associated with it, a clear protocol for accomplishing a clear mission. The organization is designed to develop leaders. In contrast, civilian leaders may or may not be trained . . . leadership roles are often earned on the basis of good performance over time. The lack of standardized training, philosophy, and role definition in civilian environments means leadership can look a hundred different ways, most of which are not recognizable as leadership to former service members.

Understanding this basic reality is essential to calibrating expectations on both sides. Retiring military personnel are best served by refraining from standing in judgment of what they see in the civilian world . . . in other words, rather than observing how ineffective things are, they should observe, with the curiosity of a sociologist, how interesting things are. My advice to former officers is that when you see something that makes no sense, rather than thinking (or saying), "That's crazy—they don't know what they're doing," instead try thinking (or saying), "Hmm, this is something I obviously don't know about . . . after all, these aren't stupid people running the show." By looking at civilian operations *in context* of civilian goals and norms rather than in a military context, former service members can reduce their exasperation factor severalfold.

Closing Thoughts

Because of the leadership culture inherent in the military, it can come as quite a shock to retired officers when they discover that civilian organizations may not have a clear leadership philosophy. To the contrary, some organizations revisit the subject of leadership on a regular basis. *It is imperative that the veteran recognize the dynamic nature of organi-*

zational strategy as not necessarily wrong or bad. Civilian organizations exist in a completely different realm from the military because they have to stay competitive/profitable in a constantly changing market-place. This fact alone creates an imperative for flexible, "agile" struc-tures and methods that can anticipate the subtlest of shifts. Explaining this concept is part of shaping expectations at the begin-ning of a veteran's employment. Other new-hires coming from indus-try may already have experience with it.

Coaching Conversation: Interpersonal Style

In this scenario, military new-hire Chris sits down with his Human Resources manager to express frustration with peer feedback.

HR Manager (HRM): Thanks for coming in, Chris, I'm glad you wanted to talk about what's happening on the team. I don't know a lot about it and look forward to hearing your perspective. How would you describe the current situation?

Chris: Well, to be honest with you, I don't really understand it myself. It seems like everything I do and say is wrong, and every-one feels the need to tell me about it. It's getting old.

HRM: Can you give me a for-instance?

Chris: Perfect example: yesterday we're in a peer work session discussing how to approach a problem for a client. It was two hours of going around and around, getting nowhere. I knew ex-actly what we should do because I've done it a hundred times in the military, but no one wanted to hear it—they just waited until I finished, then continued as if I hadn't said anything! I expected more professionalism out here in the civilian world. Yesterday was the last straw; I went back to my desk and called an Army buddy who's working over at ____ Company and loving it.

HRM: I hear your frustration. What feedback have you received about it from others?

Chris: Oh—get this—as I'm leaving the meeting, my counterpart from another team says in passing, "You're going to have to learn to play better with others if you want them to listen to you." What does that mean? I didn't come here to play, I came here to get a job done.

HRM: Anything else?

Chris: No, I never have these issues with my staff. They love me.

HRM: I'd like to be able to visualize the scenario—can you recall exactly what you said in the meeting that seemed to go unnoticed?

Chris: Sure, I said exactly what I always say, "You guys are going about this all wrong. When I was in the military we dealt with this type of breakdown all the time. Here's what we need to do. . . ." Then I told them what we need to do. Easy.

HRM: How does the *feedback* about your impact align with your *intended* impact?

Chris: It doesn't. They don't get it. I am being as clear as I know how to be, I have the solution they say they want and we could have been done with this issue last week if they just listened. I don't see the point of all these meetings to discuss a problem that has an obvious solution.

HRM: I can see that you are communicating clearly . . . it just doesn't seem to be effective. What do you make of that?

Chris: I have no idea. Everyone says, "we value honesty and integrity here," but they don't seem to be able to handle a direct conversation. One time recently, two people who agreed with me in the meeting later sent me emails back-pedaling, suggesting a different approach.

HRM: That is its own kind of feedback. What connection do you see between the various feedback you've received over the last few months since you started working here?

Chris: Obviously I'm doing something wrong, but can't figure out what it is.

HRM: Putting yourself in the shoes of these colleagues, how could your communication have come across? Think about it for a second.

[Pause]

Chris: Maybe too direct.

HRM: What have you noticed about the organization that can explain the gap between your intention and the end result?

Chris: I've noticed that people are very polite and formal here, even at the expense of efficiency. Seems like a lack of honesty to me, like they care more about being liked than about getting the job done.

HRM: What approaches have you observed others using effectively in this environment?

Chris: I'm always impressed by Joe. Everyone likes him and he still gets results. I don't know how he does it.

HRM: It's really helpful to have someone like Joe to observe. Try to put your finger on it—what do you see him doing that might shed some light on his effectiveness?

[Pause]

Chris: He asks a lot of questions. And he's very nice to people even when they make off-the-wall comments. I don't know if I'd have the patience for that.

HRM: Why do you suppose asking questions and being patient with off-the-wall comments would be important?

Chris: It seems to get people talking and moving forward. But a lot slower than just telling them what to do.

HRM: I wonder why a peer group would respond so differently to you than your direct reports. What do you make of that?

Chris: I guess my peers don't want to be told what to do. And, given that I'm sitting here with you now says something. What should I do? I don't want to dumb myself down just to play nice.

HRM: Well, you have a clear example of another approach that seems to work: Joe's approach. What would you be willing to do differently to achieve a better result?

Chris: I guess I could try asking more questions . . . and not shutting people down when they make strange comments. I'd be willing to try it and see how it goes, I guess.

HRM: That sounds like a good start. Try to notice if people respond to you differently as a result. Will you let me know how it goes?

Chris: Sure. I have another peer work session next week—I'll try it out and call you afterwards.

HRM: Is there anyone in the group who you'd feel comfortable checking in with after the meeting to get some real-time feedback?

Chris: I think I could ask Joe. He's the only one who actually acknowledges my comments anyway!

HRM: Sounds like a plan. Oh—by the way—if you like the results you get, you might consider using the same approach with your direct reports. You may be surprised by their creative problem solving skills!

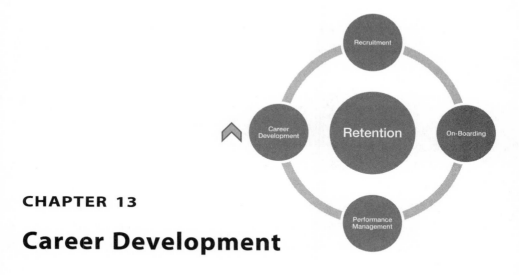

CHAPTER 13

Career Development

"In the civilian organization I encountered something for the
first time I'd never encountered in the military. And that was that
there were a number of people, a fairly large number of people,
who were there for a job and not a career."
—Officer, USMC[1]

WE HAVE COME TO THE FOURTH AND FINAL quadrant of the Veteran Retention Lifecycle: career management. Where the previous stage, performance management, focused on accelerating performance and
articulating performance metrics, this stage focuses on the new re-
quirement that the veteran take charge of his or her career. In the
military, the hierarchy was completely transparent and predictable: no
level jumping and a clear path of promotion with articulated expectations of rate of progression. The system ran the process, and the service member was part of that process, not actively engaged in politics,
positioning, or gaming the system. It was highly routinized to accommodate the huge size of the organization and, in some ways, could be
called paternalistic in that an individual's career path was taken care

of by the system. Now the service member is in a position to shape and drive his or her own career. This is an exhilarating adventure for many, but most veterans will, at some point, find it a bit mysterious.

Career Management and Retention

The most common mistake I see civilian organizations make is allowing these valuable hires to walk away too easily. Let me explain what I mean. An organization that wants to retain great talent takes the long view, recognizing that some hires may not be a good fit in their jobs. If, on the other hand, they are a good fit for the organization in general, you'll want to retain them. In addition to you as line or HR manager setting realistic expectations, the key to retaining veterans as an asset to your organization (not just the specific job/team/division they are in) is ensuring they understand internal career options. If you assume that some percentage of valued new-hires will leave their jobs within one to thirty-six months, wouldn't you rather move them internally than lose them altogether?

The most important message you can give to military new-hires is, "We value you and we want you to stay with us for a long time. As part of this corporate commitment to you as a valued member of the organization, we want you to know that there are lots of ways to be successful and happy here, so look here first before considering leaving." I'm not suggesting you read this quote to every new-hire, but it is a perspective you need to have if you want to retain veterans (or anyone, for that matter). While serving in the military, walking off the job was not an option; it was considered a crime. Now, for the first time in their careers, former service members can exercise their right to choose. Recognize this as a possibility (as you should for all employees) and reduce risk by being transparent about career options across your organization.

Another place where you as an organizational leader can directly impact retention of veterans is ongoing contact throughout the em-

FIGURE 13.1

Putting It All Together
Developing Careers in Your Organization

What are the norms and expectations related to career development in your organization? For example, is it expected that employees will aggressively drive their careers or is it more favorable to work quietly behind the scenes?

_____

_____

_____

_____

_____

What tips can you offer military new-hires to help them avoid pitfalls related to career development in your organization?

_____

_____

_____

_____

_____

ployee lifecycle. Often, an individual or group of internal Human Resources professionals serve as a point of continuity for the veteran. Oftentimes line managers also play this role. Invest in the relationship with veterans by maintaining connections over time. The most common complaint I hear from former service members is, "You can sink or swim out there, nobody cares. No one tells you how to be successful." Is this the workplace legacy you want to see embedded? Of course not.

What resources or forums does your organization have for conveying information about career paths and career advancement? Is it sufficient?

By glimpsing the military world, you have valuable insight as to what new-hires will need, whether they are aware of it or not. For veterans, managing their own careers will be a big learning curve with a lot appearing to be at stake (i.e., their civilian career). The military community is well-networked and very generous about sharing leads and information. But when it comes to giving career advice, it may well be "the blind leading the blind." Why leave retention to chance; you can make a bottom-line difference by anticipating, informing, and staying connected to the veterans you hire.

The Politics of Career Management

As with so many other topics we've covered in this book, organizational culture plays a role in career management. It's called politics, the written and unwritten rules of the road, insiders' knowledge. You should assume insider knowledge will be unknown to the military new-hire. Even after some period of tenure, if an individual hasn't given or received a promotion, chances are he or she doesn't know the nuances that go into such a decision. For example, some organizations want employees to be up-front about their career goals. Other organizations want to know their employees are ambitious, but they don't want to hear about it. Every culture is different, and we've already looked at some of the differences found in the military's transparent approach to career progression.

> "There's an expectation in the military that you're going to get promoted, that you want to advance. We don't let people stagnate. But on the civilian side, you have a lot of people who are very happy being individual contributors. They're happy being whatever level they are, and that's where they want to stay. They're not going to go out of their way to get more training or to do

something more, because they don't have any desire to advance, and so understanding what motivates people in that sector is different from the true military."

—Officer, US Army[2]

Closing Thoughts

The chart in Figure 13.2 illustrates the relationship between the four stages of the Veteran Retention Lifecycle™ and the Military Transition Framework™ discussed in Part 2 of the book.

As you may have already figured out for yourself, most service members will be in the process of detaching when you meet them in the recruitment stage. If they have had previous civilian jobs, they may be further along or finished with detaching when they interview with

FIGURE 13.2

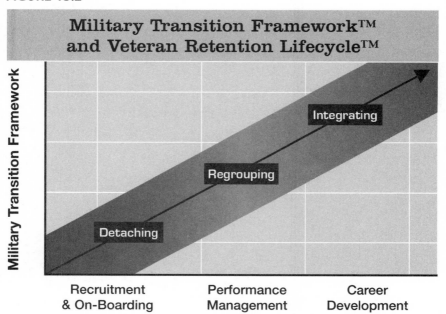

you. Regardless of where they are relative to detaching, they are thrust into regrouping as soon as on-boarding begins. Of course, regrouping will be smoother and quicker if they've completed the internal process of detaching, but the reality is that we don't know where they'll be on this score because it is a deeply personal process they may or may not be aware of themselves. Regrouping continues through the performance management stage of the lifecycle, and integration is where career development generally comes into play.

CHAPTER 14

Veteran Retention Lifecycle™ and Re-engagement

WE'VE SPENT THE PREVIOUS PAGES TALKING about the Employee Retention Lifecycle. Hopefully you've learned a lot and seen how the four stages impact one another. Each provides an opportunity to engage or intervene. Here's what I mean. When it comes to retention, we have to look *across* the employee lifecycle and *within* each stage. Recruitment, onboarding, performance management, and career management present challenges and opportunities for us as leaders and to veterans as employees. If mishandled or neglected, any one of these stages of an employee's experience with your organization can be the one in which he or she decides to opt out. When done right, any stage can be a point of engagement or re-engagement. A few examples from real life:

- *Recruitment.* Due to a misunderstanding in the hiring process, Steve assumed the full cost of his relocation would be paid for by his new employer. Imagine his dismay and disillusionment when part of the expense was denied. This left a bitter taste in his mouth for some time, causing him to wonder if he had been the victim of a bait and switch. As his first few months went by, *Steve became re-engaged* as a fan of the organization when it sponsored him in a technical certification course.

- *On-boarding.* Jean was one of those people I mentioned earlier, who was left standing awkwardly in the lobby on her first day of employment like someone showing up to a party they weren't invited to. Disorganized administrative processes continued to plague her first week of employment, leading her to wonder what she'd signed up for. These thoughts were quickly forgotten, however, during the top-shelf orientation training class Jean attended the following week. All she learned about the organization and the positive connections she made with fellow new-hires during the program *erased any doubt* she may have had about her decision to sign on.

- *Performance management.* Ideally, employee performance reviews should hold no unpleasant surprises. Unfortunately, in the real world they often do. Dale was shocked by feedback he received after what he considered a great first year with the firm. Regardless of whether it was his manager's conflict avoidance or his own defensive reaction to criticism, Dale did not expect to hear that he had missed the mark on work quality. He always met his deadlines, but, as he learned, sometimes at the expense of the end product. In the course of the performance review, Dale and his manager both realized they had made assumptions about priorities. With some frustration, they got onto the same page and agreed to move forward in a positive direction. A year later, this was *nothing more than a "war story"* for Dale as he received a promotion for outstanding performance.

- *Career management.* Lorraine was discouraged after being passed over for promotion two years in a row. She understood why, but it still hurt her pride and led her to wonder where her career was going. However, because she (1) felt a strong bond with her organization and colleagues, (2) was committed to the work, and (3) otherwise felt valued and appreciated for her effort, Lorraine had a high level of engagement in spite of her disappointment. Because of her consistently positive experiences as an employee, she *did not initiate leaving for another company after being passed over,* as someone less engaged might have done.

Private sector organizations are getting on board with specialized programs and resources for their employees who are veterans. As an emerging area of interest, it is too soon to declare any program or resource a "best practice." However, it is possible to identify practices that look promising based on early results. Following are a number of promising practices I recommend to client organizations and that you can try on for size. Let me know how they work for you!

FIGURE 14.1

Promising Practices

☐ **Recruiting**
  ○ In Use: Designated resources for attracting and hiring veterans, including involvement with area military-sponsored Transition Assistance Programs (TAPs)
  ○ *Promising Practice: Optimize these recruitment efforts by training screeners and interviewers to translate a military resume, establish realistic expectations, and assess cultural fit*

☐ **On-Boarding/Engagement**
  ○ In Use: Employee affiliation or network groups, formatted in a variety of ways, with the common purpose of building a sense of community within the organization
  ○ *Promising Practice: Provide tailored on-boarding resources and training to military hires in the earliest days, to head off predictable challenges, accelerate real-time learning, and demonstrate they are valued by the organization*

☐ **Performance Management**
  ○ In Use: Structured mentoring programs that match military new-hires with more experienced veterans
  ○ *Promising Practice: Build on the momentum established initially by imbedding checkpoints before and following the performance assessment process*

☐ **Career Development**
  ○ In Use: (see previously mentioned mentoring programs)
  ○ *Promising Practice: Provide periodic information sessions*

☐ **Retention**
  ○ In Use: All practices reported above are intended to positively impact retention
  ○ *Promising Practice: Amp up your odds of retaining veterans by engaging their families.*

Before You Implement

Chances are, your organization will require a business case of some kind before it funds a program for veterans. An important part of any business case is a statement of the problem that needs to be solved or the opportunity to be seized. Before you can articulate the problem or opportunity, you will need to do some honest reflection on yourselves as an organization. The best output of this exercise will be from a cross-functional project team rather than an individual or isolated functional team. For example, you might engage a representative or two from the following:

? Learning and Development
? OD or OE
? Diversity and Inclusion
? Human Resources
? Recruiting/talent acquisition
? Line mangers
? Customer feedback
? Veterans who have been with the organization for 2–6 months

Source: ASTD InfoLine, Issue 13, 2010, by Emily King

Conclusion

TWENTY YEARS AGO, when I worked for a training company that specialized in personality testing, a class participant told me the story of his difficult transition from a career of military service to his new civilian status. I invited him to sit down with me and the owners of the company to explore the possibilities for helping others like him. It was a compelling story, but far ahead of its time, and the owners passed on developing a transition course.

Ten years ago, I encountered the challenge of military transition in another setting, the consulting firm discussed in the premise to this book. The time was right for that company and they invested in programs to make veterans successful in the organization. Shortly thereafter I sought to validate my earlier findings with other defense contractors, and I delved more deeply, making it the subject of my master's thesis. I found common pitfalls and success factors in the study of military transitions, and, perhaps most interesting, I found tangible business impacts to business outcomes. I thought about striking out on my own to help other organizations and veterans as I had done in the present organization. But the time wasn't right; there was vague interest but a lack of urgency necessary to sustain my venture.

Now the time is finally right for this topic to be raised for discussion at a national level. Employers across the country are recognizing the valuable asset veterans are to their organizations, and many recruit directly through the military community. For many of the leaders I speak with, there is a sense of doing what's right by those who have served our country in the troubled past decade, and this has created urgency to actively engage. At the same time, First Lady Michelle Obama is launching a "Community Blueprint" in support of military families, and the Department of Labor is bringing a new savvy to the needs of veterans and the organizations that employ them.

By picking up this book, you have joined a stimulating and highly relevant conversation about the value of military service members to civilian organizations and the role such organizations can and should play in their success. The rewards will come in the form of higher retention, stronger leadership pipelines, jobs for those returning from combat, and in coming together as a nation to welcome service members home.

If your organization is reluctant to hire veterans due to concerns about post-traumatic stress disorder or other combat-related injuries, be part of the team that educates, informs, and shines a light on facts where myth would otherwise prevail. If your organization wants to hire veterans but doesn't know how, let this book be a first step toward identifying a path forward. If your organization hires veterans and wants to do a better job of retaining them as valuable assets, you are now armed with tools and suggestions for leading the way to being a veteran-friendly employer of choice.

The time to act is now and the people to act is us. All the best in your efforts to hire, manage, and retain veterans!

Action Plan

Build a Foundation for Success (Chapters 1–5 and 12)

- ✔ Complete the organizational readiness assessment (ORA) in Chapter 9
- ✔ Use the completed ORA and information from Chapter 1 to articulate a business case for hiring veterans and/or your approach
- ✔ Use the business case to enroll senior-level champions
- ✔ Refine messaging about your initiative's intent and goals, with input from champions
- ✔ Use refined messaging to garner the support of hiring managers and recruiting staff
- ✔ Integrate messaging into organization's recruitment collateral
- ✔ Identify and train new-hire mentors/sponsors to assist with initial days and weeks of employment

Recruitment (Chapters 2, 6–8, and 12)

- ✔ Analyze job requisitions for possible jobs
- ✔ Train recruiters to translate a military resume, using Chapter 12

- ⊘ Train recruiters and hiring managers to effectively interview veterans, using Chapter 12 and the translator tool in Chapter 2
- ⊘ Source candidates internally (referral) and externally
- ⊘ Assign mentors/sponsors for each military new-hire
- ⊘ Brand your organization so candidates find you
  - Showcase success stories
  - Post jobs and go to job fairs
  - Provide transition support and resources
  - Sponsor an employee resource group (ERG)

On-Boarding (Chapters 2, 6–8, and 13)

- ⊘ Engage the cross-functional team used in the ORA exercise to anticipate on-boarding challenges, needs, and ideas for
  - Training (e.g., military transition program)
  - Learning aids (e.g., reading material, glossaries)
  - Resources (e.g., mentors, ERG)
  - Appropriate integration/inclusion of new-hire's significant other
- ⊘ Use the translator tool in Chapter 2 to ensure clear messaging to new-hires
- ⊘ Develop recommendations or an action plan for taking ideas to action
- ⊘ Engage champions to gain support for recommendations or action plan
- ⊘ Provide training and/or resources to line managers for participating in on-boarding efforts
- ⊘ Engage or establish an employee resource group (ERG)
- ⊘ If an ERG already exists, enroll them as subject matter experts and reviewers of your work
- ⊘ Articulate a role and process for internal mentors

⊘ Train or otherwise inform mentors as to expectations for their role

⊘ Engage Human Resources to ensure reasonable accommodations are in place on day one

⊘ Coordinate logistics to ensure the new-hire is greeted on day one and has office space, equipment, and supplies

Performance Management (Chapters 2, 6–8, and 14)

⊘ Assemble information and resources regarding performance expectations, metrics, processes

⊘ Use the coaching questions in Chapter 12 to improve performance

⊘ Provide training and/or resources to managers on using coaching questions with veterans

⊘ Standardize use of the Manager's Mid-Year Check-In™ to provide midpoint feedback

Career Development (Chapters 2 and 6–8)

⊘ Be transparent about options to move internally

⊘ Communicate clear career paths

⊘ Track career progression

Retention (Chapters 1–14)

⊘ Stay engaged

⊘ Acknowledge Veterans Day and Memorial Day

⊘ Learn from mistakes

⊘ Learn from successes

⊘ Measure retention, promotions, other signs of success

APPENDIX B

Resources

Recruitment/Sourcing

- Post jobs on relevant online sites such as:
  - www.vetsuccess.gov (U.S. Department of Veterans Affairs)
  - www.hirevetsfirst.dol.gov (U.S. Department of Labor)
  - www.careeronestop.org (U.S. Department of Labor)
  - www.military.com (Monster.com)
  - www.gijobs.com (*G.I. Jobs* Magazine)
  - www.taonline.com (Transition Assistance Online)
- Participate in job fairs geared toward service members, such as:
  - http://military.nationalcareerfairs.com
  - www.corporategray.com
  - www.sacc-jobfair.com (Service Academy Career Conferences)
  - www.hireheroesusa.org (for wounded warriors)
  - State and local military career centers
- Connect to organizations chartered to serve veterans and employers, such as:
  - Veteran's Employment & Training Service (dol.gov/vets)

- Employer Support of the Guard and Reserve (esgr.org)
- Marine for Life (m4l.usmc.mil)
- Local military base offices of transition
- The Wounded Warrior Project (woundedwarriorproject.org)
- Vocational Rehabilitation and Employment Service (vba.gov/bln.vre)
- Advertise in publications geared to past and present service members, such as:
  - *G.I. Jobs*
  - *Military Times*
  - *Military Times Edge*
  - *Stars & Stripes*
- Solicit referrals from existing employees with a military background. There's nothing better than word-of-mouth when it comes to reaching candidates who could be a fit with your organization.

Workplace Accommodations

- www.askjan.org (Job Accommodations Network)
- www.americasheroesatwork.gov
- www.Disability.gov
- www.woundedwarriorproject.org
- www.Dol.gov/vets

On-Boarding/Transition

- "On-Boarding Veterans in the Civilian Workplace," ASTD Info-Line, Vol. 27, Issue 1013 (www.astd.org)
- www.militarytransitions.biz
- www.americasheroesatwork.gov
- www.tipofthearrow.net

End Notes

Chapter 1

   1. Navy Chief Petty Officer (E-5)

Chapter 2

   1. ASTD InfoLine, "Military to Civilian Onboarding," by Emily King. Vol. 27, Issue 1013. 2010.

   2. Captain (ret)

   3. Lt. Col. (ret)

   4. Captain (ret)

   5. Lt. Col. (ret)

   6. Technical Sergeant (E-6)

   7. Lt. Col. (ret)

   8. Chief Petty Officer (E-7)

   9. Master Sergeant (E8)

  10. Chief Petty Officer (E-7)

  11. Sergeant First Class (E-7)

Chapter 3

   1. Lt. Col. (ret)

2. Petty Officer (E-5)

Chapter 4

1. From Profile of the Military Community, Office of the Deputy Assistant Secretary of Defense.
2. Master Sergeant (E-7)

Chapter 6

1. Col. (ret)
2. Col. (ret)
3. Lt. Col. (ret)
4. Master Sargeant (E-7)
5. Lt. Col. (ret)
6. Col. (ret)

Chapter 7

1. Petty Officer (E-4)
2. Petty Officer (E-5)
3. Master Sergeant (E-8)
4. Col. (ret)
5. Lt. Col. (ret)

Chapter 8

1. Lt. Col. (ret)

Chapter 10

1. Lt. Col. (ret)
2. Master Sergeant (E-8)
3. Master Sergeant (E-7)
4. Chief Warrant Officer (CW-4)
5. Petty Officer (E-4)
6. Master Sergeant (E-7)
7. Senior Chief Petty Officer (E-8)

Chapter 11

1. Master Sergeant (E-8)
2. Lt. Col. (ret)

3. Sergeant (E-5)
4. Petty Officer (E-5)
5. Staff Sergeant (E-6)
6. Petty Officer (E-5)

Chapter 12

1. Master Sergeant (E-7)
2. Chief Petty Officer (E-9)
3. Petty Officer (E-5)
4. Col. (ret)

Chapter 13

1. Lt. Col. (ret)
2. Col. (ret)

Index

About the Author

EMILY KING is a nationally recognized expert on the transition from military service to civilian employment. She has worked extensively with organizations that hire and want to retain veterans, as well as with veterans directly. Emily's business-focused approach emphasizes the role of the civilian hiring organization in making veterans successful and has directly contributed to the retention of veterans.

Prior to founding Military Transitions,™ Emily launched the successful organizational development consulting firm of King Street Associates, LLC, and spent ten years as an internal consultant and coach at the firm of Booz Allen Hamilton, leading a variety of programs and functions geared to building strong leaders and managers.

A frequent speaker and writer in the professional HR community, Emily has given presentations at national conferences of the Society of Human Resource Management (SHRM), American Society of Training and Development (ASTD), and the Multicultural Forum on Workplace Diversity. In 2010, ASTD published her primer on veterans in the workplace as a special edition of *InfoLine*. Emily has been published by *Diversity Executive*, *T&D*, and *Training* magazines. She has been featured in segments by CNN and appears regularly on WJLA's "Capital Insider" program.

She has a Master's of Science degree in Organization Development from Johns Hopkins University, as well as training as a leadership coach at Georgetown University. Emily King lives in Washington, D.C.